Ages 5-10
Reproducible!

# The SUPER-SIZED Book of Bible Coloring & Art

with BIBLE STORIES AND VERSES

ROSEKIDZ®

**The Super-Sized Book of Bible Coloring & Art**

Published by RoseKidz®
An imprint of Hendrickson Publishing Group
Rose Publishing, LLC
P.O. Box 3473
Peabody, Massachusetts 01961-3473 USA
www.hendricksonpublishinggroup.com


Managing Editor: Karen McGraw
Editorial and Production Associate: Drew McCall
Assistant Editor: Talia Messina
Cover Design: Drew McCall

ISBN: 978-1-58411-152-8
RoseKidz® reorder #R38253
RELIGION/Christian Ministry/Children

*Printed in the United States of America*
*Printed April 2020*

# Table of Contents


INTRODUCTION ........ 8

## OLD TESTAMENT

### GENESIS

The Beginning ........ 9
God Created Everything ........ 10
Plants and Trees for Food ........ 11
It Was Very Good! ........ 12
Adam and Eve ........ 13
Disobeying God ........ 14
Noah and the Ark ........ 15
The Ark Floated ........ 16
See God's Promise ........ 17
Abram Worshiped God ........ 18
Too Many Sheep ........ 19
God's Promise to Abraham ........ 20
God's Promise to Sarah ........ 21
God Hears Our Cries ........ 22
Hagar Found Water ........ 23
God's Surprise ........ 24
Isaac Trusts ........ 25
A Deceitful Plan ........ 26
Jacob Lied to His Father ........ 27
A Colorful Coat ........ 28
Favorite Son ........ 29
Trusting in God ........ 30
Saving for the Famine ........ 31
Joseph's Brothers ........ 32
Joseph, Ruler of Egypt ........ 33

### EXODUS

Miriam ........ 34
Moses in Danger ........ 35
Baby Moses ........ 36
Pharaoh's Daughter ........ 37
The Burning Bush ........ 38
Moses, Aaron, and Pharaoh ........ 39
Let My People Go ........ 40
Pharaoh and the Frogs ........ 41
The Final Plague ........ 42
Moses and the Red Sea ........ 43
Walking through the Red Sea ........ 44
Praising God through Song ........ 45
Manna from Heaven ........ 46
Water from the Rock ........ 47
Stone Tablets ........ 48
God's Laws ........ 49
A Golden Calf ........ 50

### LEVITICUS

Renewing Faith ........ 51

### NUMBERS

Sending Spies ........ 52
An Angel in the Road ........ 53

### JOSHUA

Hiding Spies ........ 54
Helping Joshua ........ 55
The Commander Instructed Joshua ........ 56
The Wall of Jericho ........ 57
The March Around Jericho ........ 58

### JUDGES

Samson and Delilah ........ 59
Samson and the Pillars ........ 60

### RUTH

A Loyal Woman ........ 61

# Table of Contents


## 1 SAMUEL

Hannah and Samuel ... 62
Samuel Learned ... 63
A Coat for Samuel ... 64
God Spoke to Samuel ... 65
The Lord Called ... 66
David the Shepherd ... 67
God Called David ... 68
God Chose David as King ... 69
David Served God ... 70
David and Goliath ... 71
David and Jonathan ... 72

## 2 SAMUEL

Anointing a King ... 73
David Showed Kindness ... 74
Nathan Spoke the Truth to David ... 75

## 1 KINGS

Solomon Asked for Wisdom ... 76
Wise King Solomon ... 77
Solomon Prayed for the Temple ... 78
Idol Worship ... 79
Delivered by Ravens ... 80
A Poor Woman Shared ... 81
The Prophets of Baal ... 82
Elijah Called Upon God ... 83
Jezebel ... 84
Elijah Hid in a Mountain ... 85

## 2 KINGS

The Faith of a Servant Girl ... 86
Naaman Was Healed ... 87
God's Word Was Found ... 88

## NEHEMIAH

Rebuilding the Wall ... 89

## ESTHER

Search for a Queen ... 90
An Audience with the King ... 91
The Queen Saved Her People ... 92

## PSALMS

Our Good Shepherd ... 93
Wonderfully Made ... 94
Praise the Lord ... 95

## DANIEL

Daniel and Friends Chose God ... 96
Healthy Food ... 97
Ordered to Worship an Idol ... 98
Thrown into a Furnace ... 99
Daniel Prays ... 100
Daniel in the Lions' Den ... 101

## JONAH

Jonah on Board ... 102
Jonah and the Big Fish ... 103
Jonah Prayed and God Answered ... 104
Jonah on the Beach ... 105

# NEW TESTAMENT

## The Gospels: Jesus' Birth & Childhood

Zechariah and Elizabeth ... 106
A Simple Couple ... 107
An Angel Appeared ... 108
A Special Angel ... 109
The Angel Visited Mary ... 110
Journey to Bethlehem ... 111
Jesus' Birthday ... 112
Jesus Is the Light of the World ... 113
The Mother of Jesus ... 114
Jesus Arrived ... 115

# Table of Contents

Part of God's Plan ... 116
An Angel Visited the Shepherds ... 117
Shepherds Hurried to Bethlehem ... 118
A Stable Instead of a Hospital ... 119
Mary Was Thoughtful and Comforting ... 120
The Magi Followed the Star ... 121
The Visit of the Magi ... 122
People Celebrated Jesus' Birth ... 123
Baby Jesus ... 124
Jesus and His Father ... 125
Jesus Grew ... 126
Jesus as a Child ... 127
Jesus Was Obedient ... 128
His Father's House ... 129
Jesus Obeyed His Parents ... 130

## The Gospels: Jesus' Ministry

Mary and Jesus Went to Market ... 131
Jesus Is the Lamb of God ... 132
Jesus Pleased God ... 133
John the Baptist ... 134
Put in Chains ... 135
Jesus Walked along the Sea of Galilee ... 136
Fishers of People ... 137
Follow Me ... 138
Jesus Made Fishermen His Disciples ... 139
Peter Went Fishing ... 140
A Net of Fish ... 141
Follow Jesus ... 142
Miracles ... 143
Wedding at Cana ... 144
The Miracle of the Wine ... 145
The Wedding Helper ... 146
A Woman at the Well ... 147
Living Water ... 148
Jesus Healed a Sick Boy ... 149
Jesus Healed a Sick Man ... 150
Nothing Without God ... 151
Friends Carried a Man on a Cot ... 152
Finding a Way ... 153
Jesus Prayed ... 154
Prayer ... 155
Do Not Worry ... 156
The House on a Rock ... 157
Foolish Man's House ... 158
Wise Man's House ... 159
Parable of the Soils ... 160
The Waves Obeyed Him ... 161
The Wind Obeyed Jesus ... 162
Jesus Asleep on the Boat ... 163
Jesus Calmed the Sea ... 164
Just Believe ... 165
A Dying Little Girl ... 166
A Little Girl Is Alive ... 167
Touched by Jesus ... 168
Teaching the Multitude ... 169
Feeding the Many ... 170
A Boy Shared His Lunch ... 171
I Can See ... 172
A Surprise Coin ... 173
Little Ones ... 174
Helping Others ... 175
A Good Neighbor ... 176
Love Your Neighbor ... 177
The Good Samaritan ... 178
Be the Samaritan ... 179
Be Kind ... 180
Jesus Visited Mary and Martha ... 181
Mary of Bethany ... 182
Martha Complained to Jesus ... 183
Our Heavenly Father ... 184
God Knows All ... 185

# Table of Contents


The Shepherd Protects His Flock ..........186
The Lost Sheep ..........187
Lost and Found ..........188
Sheep Know the Shepherd's Voice ..........189
Jesus Told a Parable ..........190
Parable of the Lost Coin ..........191
Repent ..........192
Parable of the Lost Son ..........193
The Lost Son & the Pigs ..........194
The Lost Son Returned ..........195
Martha Ran to Meet Jesus ..........196
Believe in Jesus ..........197
Lazarus Lived ..........198
Jesus Brought Lazarus Back to Life ..........199
One Came Back ..........200
A Blind Man Saw ..........201
Zacchaeus in the Crowd ..........202
Zacchaeus Saw Jesus ..........203
Zacchaeus in the Tree ..........204
Jesus Blessed the Children ..........205
Little Children ..........206
The Rich Young Ruler's Treasure ..........207
A Family Jesus Loved ..........208
Mary's Gift for Jesus ..........209
Honor Jesus ..........210


## The Gospels: Jesus' Last Days


Jesus Entered Jerusalem ..........211
The Triumphal Entry ..........212
A Crowd Greeted Jesus ..........213
Jesus Forgave Us ..........214
The Upper Room ..........215
The Last Supper ..........216
The Garden of Gethsemane ..........217
Peter Denied Knowing Jesus ..........218
Jesus on Trial ..........219
Jesus Died and Came Alive Again ..........220
The Crucifixion ..........221
The Garden Tomb ..........222
An Angel on the Stone ..........223
Jesus Is Alive! ..........224
An Angel Announced His Resurrection ..........225
Bribed with Money ..........226
Jesus and Mary in the Garden ..........227
Jesus Appeared to His Disciples ..........228
Fishing in the Sea of Galilee ..........229
Breakfast by the Sea ..........230
The Ascension ..........231
Jesus Went Home ..........232


## ACTS


The Church Began ..........233
The Holy Spirit Came to a Secret Room ..........234
Peter and John Went to Pray ..........235
Peter Healed a Crippled Beggar ..........236
Sharing Everything ..........237
Ananias Lied to God ..........238

# Table of Contents


Sapphira Lied to God ........ 239
Saul Obeyed God ........ 240
Ananias Followed Instructions ........ 241
Saul Escaped ........ 242
Dorcas Was a Wonderful Person ........ 243
Dorcas Was Loved by Many ........ 244
Peter Healed Dorcas ........ 245
Spreading the Word ........ 246
Peter Knocked on the Door ........ 247
Peter Entered Mary's House ........ 248
Paul Told about Jesus ........ 249
Lydia Believed in Jesus ........ 250
Lydia Shared with Missionaries ........ 251
Paul Told about God ........ 252

ROMANS

We Are Children of God ........ 253

1 TIMOTHY

Jesus Is King of Our Hearts ........ 254

# Introduction

## An awesome combination!

Kids and coloring books are a natural combination. That's why *The Super-Sized Book of Bible Coloring & Art* is so awesome! It's a big book filled with coloring pages about the most exciting Bible stories for kids.

## The perfect way to learn the Bible.

Yes, kids love coloring books. Coloring spurs creativity and stimulates the imagination. Coloring books are relaxing yet educational. They allow the mind to focus and play at the same time. This is why *The Super-Sized Book of Bible Coloring & Art* is so incredible. Children will absorb each Bible story as they color the wonderful pictures.

## It's so fun they won't know they're learning!

Each page has a memory verse and brief Bible story. Parents or teachers of younger children can read and explain each story while children concentrate on coloring. Older children can read the stories and color the corresponding pictures, and they can skip around and learn the stories in any order they wish.

## The obvious advantage of this book is that it's super-sized.

Kids will never get tired of coloring these pages because there are hundreds to choose from.

- Duplicate the reproducible pages and use them again and again..
- Choose from a variety of Bible story images—some for younger children and some for older kids.
- Challenge kids to use their imaginations. Beyond basic stay-within-the-lines coloring, this book includes color-by-number, color codes, and finish-the-picture style coloring pages.
- Find Bible stories in order, from Old Testament to New Testament.
- Use a variety of coloring utensils including crayons, colored pencils, or fine-tipped felt pens.

## This book will provide hours of wholesome coloring fun!

# The Beginning

## Memory Verse

*In the beginning God created the heavens and the earth.* Genesis 1:1

## God's Creation (Genesis 1)

God's creation is filled with many wonderful things. God created everything!
Color the picture of God's creations.

# God Created Everything

## Memory Verse

*Let the waters beneath the sky flow together into one place, so dry ground may appear.* Genesis 1:9

## God Created the World (Genesis 1:1–2:3)

God created the heavens and the Earth. God made the whole world and everything in it, including you! What are some things God made? Yes, rocks, apples, lizards. Color the picture of some things God made.

# Plants and Trees for Food

## Memory Verse

*Let the land sprout with vegetation.* Genesis 1:11

## Food for Life (Genesis 1:11–29)

God created seed-bearing plants and trees on the land that bear fruit with more seeds so they would reproduce. God made all these plants and fruits for humans to use as food. Color the food below. Then, draw and color some other foods you like to eat.

# It Was Very Good!

## Memory Verse

*God created human beings in his own image.* Genesis 1:27

## God Created Adam and Eve (Genesis 1:1–31 & 2:4–25)

God created the whole world in six days! He created the day, night, sky, sun, moon, stars, land, seas, plants, trees, birds, fish, and animals. Then God formed a man from the dirt of the earth, breathed air into his lungs to give him life, and called him Adam. Next, God created a woman. He called her Eve.

Fill in the background around Adam and Eve by drawing things like trees, plants, and flowers. Then draw some of God's creatures. Color the picture.

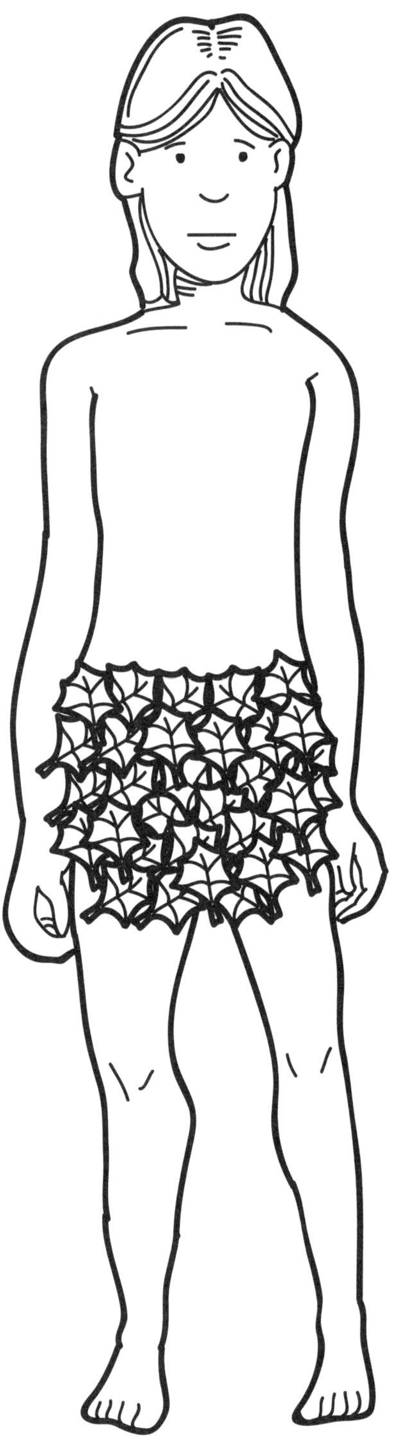

# Disobeying God

## Memory Verse

*She saw that the tree was beautiful and its fruit looked delicious . . .*
*So she took some of the fruit and ate it.* Genesis 3:6

## Adam and Eve (Genesis 3)

God told Adam and Eve to eat the fruit from all of the trees in the Garden of Eden except one. Satan became a snake and talked Eve into eating from that tree. Adam ate some, too. God was very unhappy with Adam and Eve because they did not obey him.

Draw some fruit on the tree and draw a snake wrapped around the tree.
Color the picture of Adam and Eve in the Garden of Eden.

# Adam and Eve

## Memory Verse

*This one is bone from my bone, and flesh from my flesh!* Genesis 2:23

## A Garden Home (Genesis 2:4—3:24)

Adam and Eve were the first people God made. God made a beautiful garden where they lived. It had everything they needed. God told Adam and Eve not to eat the fruit on one very special tree. A wicked snake came and told Eve to eat the fruit. Eve ate the fruit, and so did Adam. God was very unhappy with Adam and Eve. God punished Adam and Eve by sending them away from their garden home.

Color the picture of Adam and Eve in their garden home. Draw some fruit on the tree and draw a snake under the tree.

# Noah and the Ark

## Memory Verse

*Bring a pair of every kind of animal—a male and a female—into the boat with you to keep them alive during the flood.* Genesis 6:19

## God's Rainbow Promise (Genesis 6:8–8:22)

God told Noah to build a big boat called an ark. God told him to take his family and a pair of every kind of animal into the ark. God wanted to protect them from a great flood that would kill all the other people and animals. When the flood was over, Noah, his family, and the animals came out. God put a rainbow in the sky and promised he would never again kill all living things with a flood.

Color the picture of the boat. Then color the rainbow. Use lots of pretty colors.

# Abram Worshiped God

## Memory Verse

*Abram built an altar there and dedicated it to the Lord, who had appeared to him.* Genesis 12:7

## Abram Built an Altar (Genesis 12:1–8)

The Lord told Abram (who was later named Abraham) to take his family, leave his country, and move to an unknown land called Canaan. God made a promise with Abram that he would make a great nation from his family in this new land. When Abram arrived in Canaan, God appeared to him and told him that this was the land he was giving to his children's children. Abram then built an altar out of rocks and dirt to worship God.

# Too Many Sheep

## Memory Verse

*Let's not allow this conflict to come between us.* Genesis 13:8

## Abram Made Peace with Lot (Genesis 13:1–12,14,18)

Abram, his wife, and his nephew Lot moved to a land called Canaan. Abram and Lot had flocks and herds of animals. The land couldn't feed all of the animals, so the workers began fighting over the land. To keep the peace, Abram decided to divide the land. Abram gave Lot the first choice of which land he wanted. Lot chose the land he thought was the best. God was pleased with Abram for keeping the peace.

Color the picture of Abram, Lot, and their many sheep.

# God's Promise to Abraham

## Memory Verse

*The LORD took Abram outside and said to him, "Look up into the sky and count the stars if you can. That's how many descendants you will have!"* Genesis 15:5

## Promised Many Descendants (Genesis 15:5)

Abraham felt sad. He did not have any children. One day, God took Abraham outside his tent and told him to look up into the night sky. Abraham looked up and saw millions of twinkling stars. Then God promised that Abraham would have as many children, grandchildren and great-grandchildren as there were stars. Even though it seemed impossible, Abraham believed in God's promise.

Use a yellow crayon to draw enough dots to fill up the sky with stars. When you're finished, try to count how many stars you made. Are there too many to count? Now you know how Abraham felt when God told him how many relatives he would have.

# God's Promise to Sarah

## Memory Verse

*God can be trusted to keep his promise.* Hebrews 10:23

## God Gave Sarai a New Name (Genesis 17:15–21)

Names are important to God. He likes to give his followers new names. He gave Abram the new name *Abraham* after telling him that he would become the father of many nations. Then God gave his wife Sarai a new name. She became *Sarah*, which means *princess*. He also promised Sarah that she would give birth to a son, even though she was old. What God promised came true, and Sarah gave birth to Isaac.

# God's Surprise

## Memory Verse

*Abraham looked up and saw a ram caught by its horns in a thicket.* Genesis 22:13

## The Boy Who Trusted God (Genesis 22:1–19)

Isaac was a very special boy who loved and trusted God. One day, God told Isaac's father, Abraham, "Take your son and offer him as a burnt offering to me." Abraham took Isaac high on a mountain where he built an altar of stone. Then he tied Isaac's hands and feet. Just as Abraham was ready to sacrifice his son, God stopped him. In a nearby bush, there was a ram for a sacrifice instead. God knew that Abraham and Isaac really trusted in him.

Color the spaces that have a letter black. Color spaces that have a number white.

# Isaac Trusts

## Memory Verse

*The Lord will provide.* Genesis 22:14

## The Lord Will Provide (Genesis 22:1–18)

Abraham was ready to sacrifice his only son, Isaac, because he wanted to obey God. He loved God. Isaac also wanted to obey God. Instead of Abraham giving up Isaac, God gave them a ram to sacrifice. God saw that Abraham and Isaac loved him. He provided for them.

Color the picture of Abraham and Isaac finding the ram.

# A Deceitful Plan

## Memory Verse

*Don't lie to each other.* Colossians 3:9

## Rebekah Made a Stew (Genesis 27:1–13)

Rebekah was the mother of Esau and Jacob. She favored Jacob and wanted his father Isaac to give Jacob the family's blessing instead of Esau. Rebekah helped Jacob trick Isaac by making him a delicious meal. While Rebekah was cooking, Esau was out hunting so he could prepare his own meal for his father and receive the blessing. But Rebekah and Jacob had another plan.

# Jacob Lied to His Father

## Memory Verse

*Let us tell our neighbors the truth.* Ephesians 4:25

## Animal Fur (Genesis 27:13–40)

Jacob lied to his sick and blind father, Isaac, by pretending he was his brother, Esau. He wanted the blessing that Esau was supposed to get. To fool his father, Jacob wore his brother's clothes and brought his father the tasty stew that Rebekah had made. He even put animal fur on his arms because Esau was a hairy man. Isaac didn't believe Jacob was really Esau until he felt his hairy arms. Isaac ate the stew and gave Jacob the blessing instead of Esau.

Draw animal fur on Jacob's arms.

# A Colorful Coat

## Memory Verse

*Israel loved Joseph more than any of his other children.* Genesis 37:3

## Joseph & the Coat of Many Colors (Genesis 37:3–4)

Joseph was a boy who loved God. God blessed Joseph and helped him. Joseph took care of his father's sheep. Because Joseph's father loved him very much, he gave Joseph a beautiful coat made with many colors.

Follow the numbers to color Joseph's coat. Then color the sheep and add a desert landscape.

1 = Red

2 = Yellow

3 = Blue

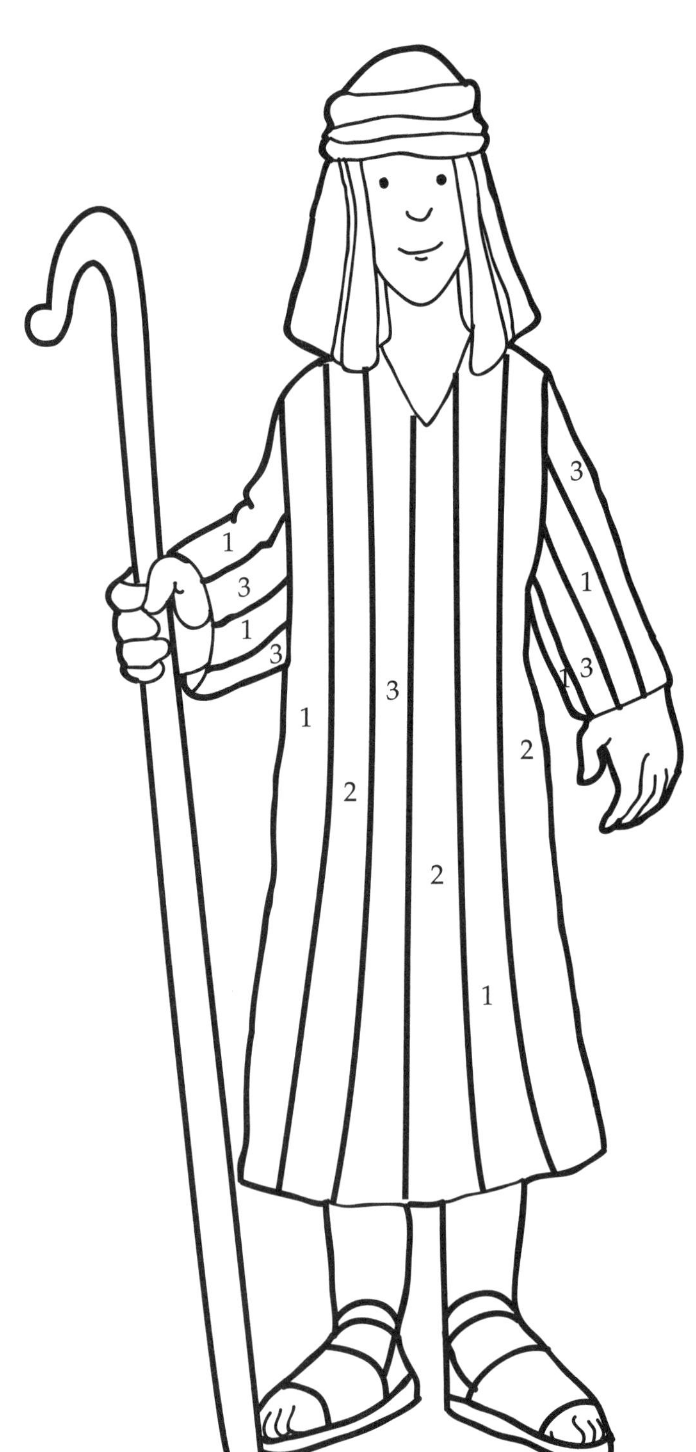

# Favorite Son

## Memory Verse

*His brothers hated Joseph because their father loved him more than the rest of them.* Genesis 37:4

## Jacob and Joseph (Genesis 37:3–4)

Jacob had twelve sons, but he loved Joseph the most and made Joseph a very colorful coat. Joseph's brothers were jealous of Joseph because of his father's favor toward him.

Color the picture of Jacob and Joseph. Include many colors on Joseph's coat.

# Trusting in God

## Memory Verse

*The Lord was with Joseph, so he succeeded.* Genesis 39:2

## Joseph Goes to Jail (Genesis 39:1–23)

Joseph was sold by his brothers and became a slave to Potiphar, who was a guard for Pharaoh, the king of Egypt. Potiphar noticed that God blessed everything that Joseph did. One day, when Potiphar was away, his wife wanted Joseph to do something for her. Joseph knew that God would not approve, so he said no and left. Potiphar's wife got mad at Joseph. She lied about Joseph to Potiphar when he came home. Joseph was taken to jail even though he had done nothing wrong. But the Lord was with Joseph and protected him in jail.

Color a picture of the scene below.

# Saving for the Famine

## Memory Verse

*The seven years of famine began, just as Joseph had predicted.* Genesis 41:54

## The Famine Begins (Genesis 41:28–57)

Joseph lived in Egypt. He was 30 years old when Pharaoh put him in charge of the people. God showed Pharaoh in a dream that a famine was coming. A famine is when there isn't enough food to eat. The famine would last seven years. Joseph showed the Egyptians how to save some of their food. Only Egypt had enough food because the people had listened to Joseph. Joseph got his wisdom from God.

Color the picture of Joseph showing the people how to save food. Draw some corn in Joseph's hand.

# Miriam

## Memory Verse

*The Lord is my light and my salvation.* Psalm 27:1

## The Little Baby (Exodus 1—2:9)

Miriam had a new baby brother. She loved her baby brother very much, but he was in danger. Pharaoh wanted to kill all the Israelite baby boys. To keep her baby brother safe, Miriam and her mother placed the baby in a basket and sent it down the river. Miriam followed the basket. When the Pharaoh's daughter found the baby, Miriam suggested her mother help care for the child. God protected this special baby boy.

Color the scene below.

# Moses in Danger

## Memory Verse

*Moses was born—a beautiful child in God's eyes.* Acts 7:20

## A Mother Hides Her Baby (Exodus 2:1–4)

The Israelite mothers were frightened. The Egyptian king had ordered that all the boys born to the Israelites should be killed. Moses' mother made a basket and prepared it so it would not sink. She put her baby inside and hid the basket in the reeds along the river. Miriam, the baby's sister, kept watch.

Use the color key to color the spaces.

1 = blue • 2 = brown • 3 = green • 4 = yellow

# Baby Moses

## Memory Verse

*She put the baby in the basket and laid it among the reeds along the bank of the Nile River.* Exodus 2:3

## A Secret Hiding Place (Exodus 2:1–10)

Moses was a very special baby. To keep him safe from a bad king, Moses' family hid him in a basket on the river. Moses' sister, Miriam, hid in the reeds to be sure Moses was safe. A kind princess found Moses' basket bed and took him home with her.

Color the picture. Make sure to use bright orange or yellow to color the sun in the sky.

# Pharaoh's Daughter

## Memory Verse

*The princess named him Moses, for she explained, "I lifted him out of the water."* Exodus 2:10

## Moses Is Found (Exodus 2:1–10)

When Moses was a baby, his mother hid him from Pharaoh inside a basket she made and carefully set it in the reeds on the Nile River. When Pharaoh's daughter came to bathe in the Nile, she saw the basket and sent a slave to get it. Moses grew up in the palace as Pharaoh's grandson!

# Let My People Go

## Memory Verse

*This is what the LORD says: Let my people go.* Exodus 8:1

## God Sent the Plagues (Exodus 7:14—11:10)

God sent Moses and his brother Aaron to Egypt to lead his people to a new land. Pharaoh, the king of Egypt, wouldn't let God's people leave. Each time Moses and Aaron told Pharaoh to let God's people go, he said no. Each time Pharaoh said no, God sent a plague. The Nile River turned to blood. God sent frogs, gnats, flies, hail, and locusts. The Egyptians' animals died, and people were covered with boils. God sent darkness for three days. Still, Pharaoh said no.

Color the picture of Pharaoh, Moses, and the plagues.

# Pharaoh and the Frogs

## Memory Verse

*Frogs overran the land and even invaded the king's bedrooms.* Psalm 105:30

## Frogs Everywhere (Exodus 8:1–6)

To convince Pharaoh to let the Israelites leave Egypt, God caused ten plagues. One of these was a plague of frogs. Frogs covered all of the land in Egypt. They were everywhere! There was no place in Egypt that was not jumping with frogs. But as bad as the frogs were, Pharaoh still would not allow the Israelites to leave Egypt. It took all ten plagues to convince him to let them go.

Color the picture of frogs jumping on Pharaoh's bed.

# The Final Plague

## Memory Verse

*The people of Israel did just as the* LORD *had commanded.* Exodus 12:28

## Protected by God (Exodus 12:21–30)

The last and final plague of Egypt was the death of every Egyptian family's firstborn son. God provided the Israelites protection from this terrible plague. Through Moses, God commanded the Israelites to paint lambs' blood on their doors. When the angel of death went through the land of Egypt, he passed over the homes with blood on the doors.

# **Moses and the Red Sea**

## Memory Verse

*Moses raised his hand over the sea, and the LORD opened up a path through the water with a strong east wind.* Exodus 14:21

## The Sea Parted (Exodus 14)

When Moses led God's people out of Egypt, they camped near the Red Sea. Pharaoh's army was coming after them, and they had nowhere to go. But God was faithful and divided the sea waters so the Israelites could cross on dry land to the other side.

Color the scene below.

# Walking through the Red Sea

## Memory Verse

*The people of Israel walked through the middle of the sea on dry ground, with walls of water on each side!* Exodus 14:22

## Water on Both Sides (Exodus 14:19–22)

God protected the Israelites with a huge miracle. He parted the waters of the Red Sea and, with a wall of water on their left side and on their right side, they walked through the middle.

# Praising God through Song

## Memory Verse

*I will sing to the Lord, for he has triumphed gloriously.* Exodus 15:1

## Moses Leads in Song and Thanksgiving (Exodus 15:1–18)

Immediately after the Israelites walked through the Red Sea to the other side, they sang for joy. They had much to be thankful for because God delivered them from the Egyptians.

Color the scene below.

# Manna from Heaven

## Memory Verse

*They ate manna until they came to the border of the land of Canaan.* Exodus 16:35

## God Cared for the Israelites (Exodus 16)

When the Israelites were traveling through the desert after escaping from the Egyptians, they started grumbling because they had no food. So God provided them with manna every day. Manna was like frost that appeared on the ground. The Israelites gathered it and made tasty food out of it.

# Water from the Rock

## Memory Verse

*Strike the rock, and water will come gushing out. Then the people will be able to drink.* Exodus 17:6

## Water Gushed Forth (Exodus 17:1–7)

Moses led the Israelites through the desert. They camped at a place named Rephidim, but there was no water to drink. God told Moses to strike a rock with his staff. Miraculously, water gushed forth. God was faithful to the Israelites.

Draw the water coming out of the rock and color the picture.

# Stone Tablets

## Memory Verse

*The two stone tablets [were] inscribed with the terms of the covenant, written by the finger of God.* Exodus 31:18

## Moses and the Ten Commandments (Exodus 31:18)

God called Moses to the top of Mount Sinai where he gave him laws for living. The Ten Commandments were part of these laws. God wrote the Ten Commandments on two stone tablets. These commandments were given to help the people live a life that pleases God. We still follow them today!

Color the scene below.

# God's Laws

## Memory Verse

*Moses . . . held in his hands the two stone tablets inscribed with the terms of the covenant.* Exodus 32:15

## Moses Returned (Exodus 32:15–16)

After God gave Moses two stone tablets containing the Ten Commandments, he brought them down the mountain. These were laws or rules that God gave the Israelites so they could live a life that pleased him. God made these laws for our own good. Read them in Exodus 20:1-17.

Draw the stone tablets in Moses' hands, then color the picture.

# A Golden Calf

## Memory Verse

*Moses saw the calf and the dancing, and he burned with anger.* Exodus 32:19

## Worshiping a False God (Exodus 32:1–6)

While Moses was on the top of Mount Sinai receiving God's laws, the Israelites grew tired of waiting for him. Without their leader, they soon forgot that God brought them out of Egypt. Using gold jewelry, Aaron made a golden calf statue. They worshiped the idol with a big party.

# Renewing Faith

## Memory Verse

*Restore to me the joy of your salvation, and make me willing to obey you.* Psalm 51:12

## Feast of Tabernacles (Leviticus 23:33–43)

The Jewish Feast of Tabernacles celebrated the final harvest. Huts made of fresh branches, palm trees, and willows were constructed in the streets, courts, public squares, and house roofs. For seven days, families lived in these huts as a reminder of the fatherly care and protection of their Lord God when he guided them from Egypt to Canaan. Celebrations renewed their faith and taught the children about God's goodness.

# Sending Spies

## Memory Verse

*We even saw giants there . . . Next to them we felt like grasshoppers, and that's what they thought, too!* Numbers 13:33

## Giants in the Land (Numbers 13)

A spy is someone who secretly watches others without being discovered. God told Moses to send some spies to Canaan. This was the land that God had promised his people. Moses sent twelve men, including Joshua and Caleb, to search the land. He wanted to know what kinds of cities were there, how strong the people were, and what kind of fruit the land had. Ten of the spies returned very afraid of what they saw: giants and strongly-built cities. But Joshua and Caleb saw beyond the giants and knew that God could give them the power to conquer the land.

Color the scene below.

# An Angel in the Road

## Memory Verse

*Balaam's donkey saw the angel of the Lord standing in the road.* Numbers 22:23

## Listening to a Donkey (Numbers 22:16–31)

King Balak sent Balaam a message that he wanted to see him. But God didn't want Balaam to go see King Balak. As Balaam was traveling by donkey, God sent an angel to stop him. However, the donkey was the only one who could see the angel. When the donkey ran off the road, Balaam beat her. Balaam didn't understand why she wasn't cooperating with him. Finally, the donkey lay down in the road and wouldn't budge. God used the donkey to get Balaam's attention. The donkey actually spoke to Balaam. Then, his eyes were opened and he, too, saw the angel.

Color the scene below.

# Hiding Spies

## Memory Verse

*The LORD your God is the supreme God of the heavens above and the earth below.* Joshua 2:11

## Rahab and the Scarlet Cord (Joshua 2)

Joshua, the leader of the Israelite army, was planning an attack on Jericho. The city of Jericho had high walls all around it, so Joshua sent two spies to investigate. The spies stayed with a woman named Rahab in Jericho. Because she trusted God, she risked her life to hide the spies. They promised Rahab she would be safe during the attack if she put a scarlet cord in her window. When Joshua's army attacked Jericho, Rahab and her family were spared.

Color the picture of Rahab looking out her window. Make sure to color the cord red.

# Helping Joshua

## Memory Verse

*Joshua went up to him and demanded, "Are you friend or foe?"* Joshua 5:13

## Joshua and the Commander of the Lord's Army (Joshua 5:13–15)

As Joshua came near Jericho, he saw a man standing with a sword in his hand. The man told Joshua that he was the commander of the Lord's army and he had come to help Joshua. How do you think Joshua felt, knowing that he had a heavenly warrior on his side?

Draw the sword in the hand of the Lord's commander. Color the picture.

# The Commander Instructed Joshua

## Memory Verse

*The gates of Jericho were tightly shut because the people were afraid of the Israelites.* Joshua 6:1

## How to Attack (Joshua 6)

The people of Jericho were afraid of the Israelite army because they had heard about the miracles that the Israelites' God had performed. The commander of the Lord's army told Joshua that Joshua would win the battle with Jericho. He even told him exactly how to attack! Joshua obeyed the commander's instructions, and the Israelite army defeated Jericho. Color the picture.

# The Wall of Jericho

## Memory Verse

*March around the town, and the armed men will lead the way in front of the Ark of the* L*ORD.* Joshua 6:7

## Joshua and the Battle of Jericho (Joshua 6:1–20)

The city of Jericho had a big, thick stone wall around it. God told Joshua and the people that if they would obey him, he would make the wall fall down. God told Joshua to have the people march around the city. They marched and marched and marched. Then they blew their trumpets. The wall fell down!

Color the picture of Jericho.

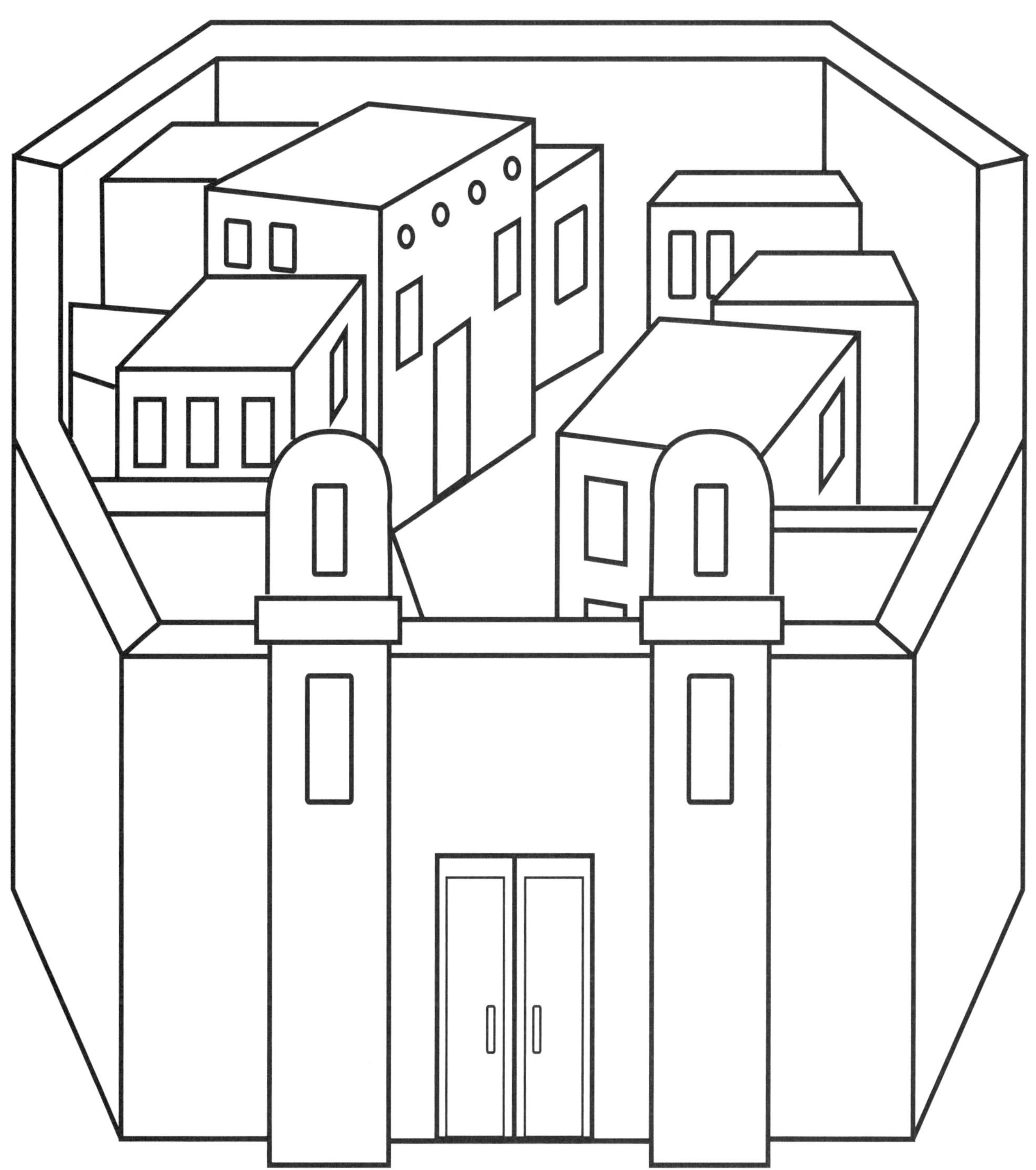

# The March Around Jericho

## Memory Verse

*The seven priests with the rams' horns marched in front of the Ark of the LORD, blowing their horns.* Joshua 6:13

## Trumpets (Joshua 6:9–20)

The Israelite army attacked Jericho by marching around the city for seven days while seven priests blew trumpets made of rams' horns. This was a strange way to attack, but because the Israelites obeyed God's commands, Jericho's walls tumbled down.

Draw a ram's horn trumpet for each priest, then color the picture.

# Samson and Delilah

## Memory Verse

*Delilah lulled Samson to sleep with his head in her lap, and then she called in a man to shave off the seven locks of his hair.* Judges 16:19

## Samson Lost His Power (Judges 16:1–22)

God gave Samson amazing strength to fight the Philistines. The Philistines wanted to know where Samson's power came from so they tricked him by offering money to Delilah to find out. Samson told Delilah that the secret was his long hair. While Samson slept, Delilah called a Philistine to shave his head. Samson was no longer strong. He was taken prisoner.

Color the picture of Samson, Delilah, and the Philistine.

# Samson and the Pillars

## Memory Verse

*Samson put his hands on the two center pillars that held up the temple. Pushing against them with both hands, he prayed.* Judges 16:29–30

## Revenge (Judges 16:23–31)

After Samson's head was shaved and all of his strength was gone, the Philistines blinded him and put him in prison. One day, the rulers called him out of prison to entertain them in their pagan temple. No one realized that his strength had returned as his hair grew back. Crying out to God one last time for strength, Samson pushed down the pillars of the temple and the building collapsed.

Draw hair, a moustache, and a beard on Samson. Color the picture.

# A Loyal Woman

## Memory Verse

*Wherever you go, I will go; wherever you live, I will live.* Ruth 1:16

## I Won't Leave You (Ruth 1)

A man named Elimelek and his wife Naomi moved to Moab to escape a famine. Elimelek died and Naomi was left with her two sons. The sons married Moabite women, one named Orpah and the other Ruth. When Naomi's two sons died, Naomi decided to move back to her homeland since the famine had ended. She told Orpah and Ruth each to return to their mother's home. Orpah left, but Ruth refused and vowed to never leave Naomi alone.

Color the scene below.

# Hannah and Samuel

## Memory Verse

*I am giving him to the LORD, and he will belong to the LORD his whole life.* **1 Samuel 1:28**

## Brought to Serve in the Temple (1 Samuel 1)

Hannah prayed to God and promised him that if she had a son, he would serve the Lord in the temple. After God gave her a son named Samuel, Hannah kept her promise to him. When Samuel was a young boy, Hannah brought him to live in the temple to help Eli, the priest. As Eli's helper, Samuel was also God's helper. He grew up to be the greatest judge that Israel ever had.

Color the picture of Eli, Samuel, and Hannah.

# Samuel Learned

## Memory Verse

*The boy served the LORD by assisting Eli the priest.* 1 Samuel 2:11

## Eli Taught Samuel (1 Samuel 1)

Samuel was Eli's helper in the tabernacle. Samuel's mother sent him there to live so he could grow up serving the Lord. Samuel was a good helper and learner. He cleaned the furniture, swept floors, and helped Eli with the sacrifices. He learned Scripture and the priest's ways by working alongside Eli. Soon, Samuel would become a prophet, and the people of Israel would listen carefully to his advice.

Color the picture of Eli and Samuel.

# A Coat for Samuel

## Memory Verse

*Each year his mother made a small coat for him and brought it to him.* 1 Samuel 2:19

## A Special Birthday Present (1 Samuel 2:18–21)

God answered Hannah's prayers and gave her a son. Hannah kept her promise that the child would grow up in the Lord's house. Each year, Hannah and her husband went to the temple to worship. At that time, Hannah would get to see Samuel. She would make a special robe for Samuel and take it to him. God blessed Hannah with many more sons and daughters, and Samuel grew up in the presence of the Lord.

Do you think he was happy or sad with his new coat? Draw a face on Samuel and color the picture.

# God Spoke to Samuel

## Memory Verse

*Speak, LORD, your servant is listening.* 1 Samuel 3:9

## Samuel Listened (1 Samuel 3:1–21)

Samuel knew that he was God's servant and wanted to obey him. Even when Samuel was a young child, God talked to him. It didn't matter to God that Samuel was just a young boy. God saw a young man who was willing to listen. Samuel's heart was important to God.

Color the picture of Samuel listening for God.

# The Lord Called

## Memory Verse

*Eli realized it was the LORD who was calling the boy.* 1 Samuel 3:8

## Samuel in the Night (1 Samuel 3)

One night when Samuel was sleeping, he heard his name called. He ran to Eli because he thought Eli called him. After Samuel heard his name called and ran to Eli three times, Eli realized the Lord was calling Samuel. The fourth time the Lord called Samuel, Samuel was ready to hear what he had to say.

Draw stars in the window and a candle on the table. Color the picture.

# David the Shepherd

## Memory Verse

*"There is still the youngest," Jesse replied. "But he's out in the fields watching the sheep and goats."* 1 Samuel 16:11

## Time Alone (1 Samuel 16:1–13)

When David was young, he worked as a shepherd for his father's flocks. Shepherds lived day and night on the hillsides with their sheep. So much time alone allowed David to think about the Lord and the beauty of his creation. David played the harp. David wrote many of the Bible's psalms.

Color David and his harp in the scene below.

# God Called David

## Memory Verse

*The Lord looks at the heart.* 1 Samuel 16:7

## God Called a Shepherd Boy (1 Samuel 16:1–13)

David watched his father's sheep. He took very good care of them. When the people needed a new king, God picked David. David made a good king because he was a good shepherd who took care of his flock. God likes it when we work hard and follow him.

Leave the spaces with *A* white. Color the spaces with *B* green. Color the spaces with *C* blue. Color the spaces with *D* brown. Color the spaces with *E* black.

# God Chose David as King

## Memory Verse

*The Spirit of the Lord came powerfully upon David from that day on.* 1 Samuel 16:13

## The Youngest Son was Chosen (1 Samuel 16:1–13)

God sent Samuel to visit Jesse and his sons because God had chosen one of them to be the next king. But God rejected all of the older sons. Then the youngest son, David, arrived. God told Samuel he was the one. God chose David because his heart was right with God, not because of his age or his looks or his height.

Color the scene below.

# David Served God

## Memory Verse

*"Don't worry about this Philistine," David told Saul. "I'll go fight him!"* 1 Samuel 17:32

## David Met a Giant (1 Samuel 17:1–51)

A giant named Goliath made fun of God and God's people. The people were afraid to fight Goliath, but David was not afraid. David knew God would help him fight Goliath. David took a slingshot and some stones, and he killed Goliath. The people were very happy God helped David defeat their enemy.

Draw a happy face on David. Draw an angry face on Goliath. Then color the picture.

# David and Goliath

## Memory Verse

*Everyone assembled here will know that the LORD rescues his people.* 1 Samuel 17:47

## David Had Courage (1 Samuel 17:1–51)

David had great courage to take on a giant. He was a young person who had faith in the Lord. God honored his faith and gave him the talent to defeat Goliath.

Draw the giant Goliath.

# David and Jonathan

## Memory Verse

*A real friend sticks closer than a brother.* Proverbs 18:24

## Good Friends (1 Samuel 18:1–4)

Jonathan was King Saul's son and a soldier in his father's army. David was a shepherd boy who proved himself a warrior by defeating Goliath. David and Jonathan became best friends. Jonathan was a true friend and helped David escape the anger of King Saul.

Color the picture of David and Jonathan.

# Anointing a King

## Memory Verse

*The men of Judah came to David and anointed him king.* 2 Samuel 2:4

## David Became King (2 Samuel 2:1–4)

The Israelites decided they wanted to have a king like the other countries did. God gave them what they wanted. He directed Samuel, the prophet, to anoint Saul as their king. At first, King Saul followed all the laws of God. When King Saul changed and began to please himself, God rejected him as king. He told Samuel to anoint David as the new king over Israel.

Color the picture of Samuel anointing David as the new king.

# David Showed Kindness

## Memory Verse

*I want to show God's kindness.* 2 Samuel 9:3

## David was Kind to Mephibosheth (2 Samuel 9)

David loved Jonathan as if he were his own brother. Jonathan had a son named Mephibosheth, who could not walk well. After Jonathan died, David searched for Jonathan's son and brought him to his palace. At first Mephibosheth was afraid because he didn't know why David called for him. David wanted to show kindness toward his friend's son. He did so by inviting Mephibosheth and his family to eat at the king's table from that day on.

Draw Mephibosheth's crutches lying on the floor beside him.

# Nathan Spoke the Truth to David

## Memory Verse

*David confessed to Nathan, "I have sinned against the LORD."* 2 Samuel 12:13

## David Realized His Mistake (2 Samuel 12:1–14)

David was a good king who did something very bad that displeased God. David didn't think what he did was wrong until Nathan, a prophet of God, talked to him about it. Nathan made David realize that he had sinned not only against another person but, most importantly, he had sinned against God. What Nathan said was true and spoken in kindness and love, which helped David realize his mistakes. Color the picture of Nathan and David.

# Solomon Asked for Wisdom

## Memory Verse

*Give me an understanding heart so that I can govern your people well and know the difference between right and wrong.* 1 Kings 3:9

## Solomon was Wise (1 Kings 3)

God appeared to Solomon and said, "Ask for whatever you want me to give you." Solomon asked only for wisdom so he could be a good ruler for his people. The wisdom granted Solomon allowed him to make good judgments.

Color the story of Solomon below.

# Wise King Solomon

## Memory Verse

*The wise are glad to be instructed.* Proverbs 10:8

## The Whole Truth (1 Kings 3:16–28)

King Solomon asked God for wisdom to rule the people. Here is an example of how wise he was. One day, two women came before the king with a baby. Each of the women said, "This is my son! Her baby died." King Solomon did not know who was the actual mother. He asked God for wisdom. "Cut the baby in two halves," Solomon ordered. "Give each woman half of the baby." One of the women said, "Good! Neither one of us will have him." The other woman cried, "No! Give the baby to her!" Wise King Solomon knew the last woman was the real mother and gave her the baby.

Draw the missing half of the baby. Then, color the picture.

# Solomon Prayed for the Temple

## Memory Verse

*May your eyes be open to my requests and to the requests of your people Israel.* 1 Kings 8:52

## Celebrating the Temple of God (1 Kings 8:62–66)

King Solomon was a wise king. During his reign, he had the temple of God built. The temple was a great and beautiful place where people prayed and worshiped God. When it was completed, King Solomon and his people celebrated by praising God and thanking him. This celebration lasted for fourteen days! King Solomon asked God for a special blessing on his people so that they would live in ways that were pleasing to him.

Color the picture of King Solomon worshiping below.

# Idol Worship

## Memory Verse

*You must not make for yourself an idol of any kind.* Exodus 20:4

## Made of Gold (1 Kings 12:25–33)

King Jeroboam ruled the northern tribes of Israel. He was a wicked king. He built two golden calves for the people to worship so they would not travel to Jerusalem to worship the Holy God of Israel. The Israelites who obeyed King Jeroboam and worshiped the idol-calves were disobeying God. The Israelites who did not worship the calves kept their hearts and minds pure and pleasing to God.

Color the picture below. Then, put a big *X* over the picture to show that God doesn't like idol worship.

# The Prophets of Baal

## Memory Verse

*They called on the name of Baal from morning until noontime . . .
But there was no reply of any kind.* 1 Kings 18:26

## Accepting a Challenge (1 Kings 18:16–29)

The people of Israel started to worship a false god named Baal. Elijah, the prophet of the one true God, wanted his people to see how wrong it was to worship Baal. So he challenged the people to make a sacrifice on their altar to their god. Elijah also would make a sacrifice, but his would be to the real God. Elijah said that the god who answered by sending fire to burn the sacrifice would be the most powerful. Baal's followers called and danced all day expecting to hear from Baal. But nothing happened, because he was not real. Color the image below.

# Elijah Called Upon God

## Memory Verse

*The fire of the LORD flashed down from heaven.* 1 Kings 18:38

## God Answered with Fire (1 Kings 18:30–40)

Elijah knew that the false god Baal would not send fire to burn the sacrifice. He wanted to show Baal's followers the power of the real God. First, he set up an altar using twelve large stones with wood on top. Then, he dug a huge ditch all the way around the altar. The sacrifice was placed on top of the wood. He poured water over the entire altar and in the ditch. Finally, Elijah prayed. God sent fire to burn the sacrifice, wood, stones, water, and even the dirt.

Draw fire coming down from heaven and burning up the altar.

# Jezebel

## Memory Verse

*[Ahab] told Jezebel everything Elijah had done.* 1 Kings 19:1

## Jezebel Sought Elijah's Life (1 Kings 19:1–8)

Jezebel was a very mean and wicked queen who served the false god Baal. Her husband was King Ahab, who was urged to do evil by his wife. Jezebel was angry that Elijah's God proved more powerful than Baal. She also was angry because Elijah had the false prophets put to death. She relied on these false prophets to make her rich. So Jezebel wanted to see Elijah put to death. She sent a messenger to tell Elijah that he would die the next day, just like Baal's prophets. Color the picture.

# Elijah Hid in a Mountain

## Memory Verse

*Go out and stand before me on the mountain.* 1 Kings 19:11

## Listening for God (1 Kings 19:9–18)

Elijah proved how mighty God was by overcoming Baal's followers. Now Queen Jezebel was angry and wanted Elijah killed. Elijah ran far away to Mount Horeb. While Elijah was there, God told him to stand on the mountain. A great storm tore the mountain apart. But God was not in the storm. Then there was an earthquake and a fire, but God was not in those either. Finally, God spoke in a gentle whisper. Elijah realized he had to be quiet and listen for God, not just look for him in mighty ways.

Draw a great storm with dark clouds and lightning. Color the picture.

# The Faith of a Servant Girl

## Memory Verse

*O Lord, if you heal me, I will be truly healed.* Jeremiah 17:14

## A Good Deed (2 Kings 5:1–5)

Naaman was a great army leader. He also had a terrible disease called leprosy, which could not be cured. Naaman's wife had a servant girl who heard about his disease. The servant girl knew of one of God's prophets, Elisha, who could heal Naaman. She told her mistress all about Elisha and the God he served. She had faith that God would help Elisha heal Naaman. The mistress told her husband the good news, and Naaman went in search of Elisha. Color the picture.

# Naaman Was Healed

## Memory Verse

*I will call on God, and the LORD will rescue me.* Psalm 55:16

## Naaman's Spots (2 Kings 5:1–16)

Naaman's servant girl was worried about her master. She told Naaman's wife about the prophet Elisha who could help Naaman. Naaman traveled far to find Elisha. Elisha told him to dip seven times into the Jordan River. When he came up after the seventh time, the spots were gone. God had healed him.

Color the picture of Naaman dipping in the Jordan River.

# God's Word Was Found

## Memory Verse

*I have found the Book of the Law in the LORD's Temple!* 2 Kings 22:8

## A Great Discovery (2 Kings 22:8—23:3)

The scroll with God's Word written in it had been lost for a long time. One day, someone found it and brought it to King Josiah. Josiah read God's Word to the people. "From now on, we will obey what God's Word says," Josiah told everyone. "We will love God and keep his laws. We will do what God wants us to do." God was happy King Josiah wanted the people to hear his Word and obey it.

Follow the color key to color the picture of King Josiah reading God's Word to the people.

# Rebuilding the Wall

## Memory Verse

*"Let's rebuild the wall!" So they began the good work.* Nehemiah 2:18

## Strength to Finish the Job (Nehemiah 6:15–16)

Nehemiah gathered everyone together to help rebuild Jerusalem's broken wall. A wall around a city was very important in Bible times for protection. God used Nehemiah as the leader to guide the people in this work. God gave them the strength to do the job and the wall was rebuilt in fifty-two days!

# Search for a Queen

## Memory Verse

*The young woman who most pleases the king will be made queen.* Esther 2:4

## Beautiful Esther (Esther 2:1–18)

King Xerxes was searching for a woman to be his next queen. Esther was very pretty. She was brought to the king as one of the women from whom he would choose for queen. The women were taken into the king's palace and given beauty treatments before they were presented to the king. Esther was a Jew, one of God's people, but she did not tell anyone, as her uncle Mordecai had instructed her. When the girls were presented to the king, he chose beautiful Esther, not knowing that she was a Jew.

# An Audience with the King

## Memory Verse

*Though it is against the law, I will go in to see the king. If I must die, I must die.* Esther 4:16

## Willing to Confront the King (Esther 4–5:7)

Esther had to approach the king to ask him to save her people. It was not easy for Esther to face the king. She knew that anyone who approached him without being asked could be put to death. Only if the king held out his gold scepter would the person live. Esther prayed for three days. Then she put on her royal robes and went to the king. The king was pleased to see her and held out his golden scepter, letting her live.

Esther dressed carefully before going to see the king. Color Esther's royal robes with the colors you think she might have worn to see the king.

# The Queen Saved Her People

## Memory Verse

*I ask that my life and the lives of my people will be spared.* Esther 7:3

## The King Listened to Esther (Esther 3–5; 7)

Haman was a very bad man. He convinced the king to make a law to kill the Jews. Mordecai, Queen Esther's uncle, told her about the law and begged her to talk to the king to stop it. Esther was a brave woman. She asked the king to save her and her people, the Jews. The king listened to Esther, and he stopped Haman's evil plan to kill the Jews. The king made another law that allowed the Jews to fight back. Esther helped save God's people, the Jews.

Draw jewelry on Esther and stones in her crown. Color the picture.

# Our Good Shepherd

## Memory Verse

*The LORD is my shepherd; I have all that I need.* Psalm 23:1

## Jesus Is Our Good Shepherd (Psalm 23)

Shepherds took very good care of the sheep in their flock. They protected them from harm and led them to good pasture. The sheep knew their shepherd and trusted him and followed him. We have Jesus as our Good Shepherd who takes care of us and guides us, but we must obey and follow him. Write your initials on one of the sheep. Color the picture.

# Wonderfully Made

## Memory Verse

*Thank you for making me so wonderfully complex! Your workmanship is marvelous.* Psalm 139:14

## God Loves You (Psalm 139)

God made wonderful things, including you. God loves you because he made you. God knows everything you do, say, and think. He even knew you before we were born! God loves you very much. In the Bible, David knew this and David praised God for making us, knowing us and loving us.

Draw a picture of your face in this outline. Color the picture.

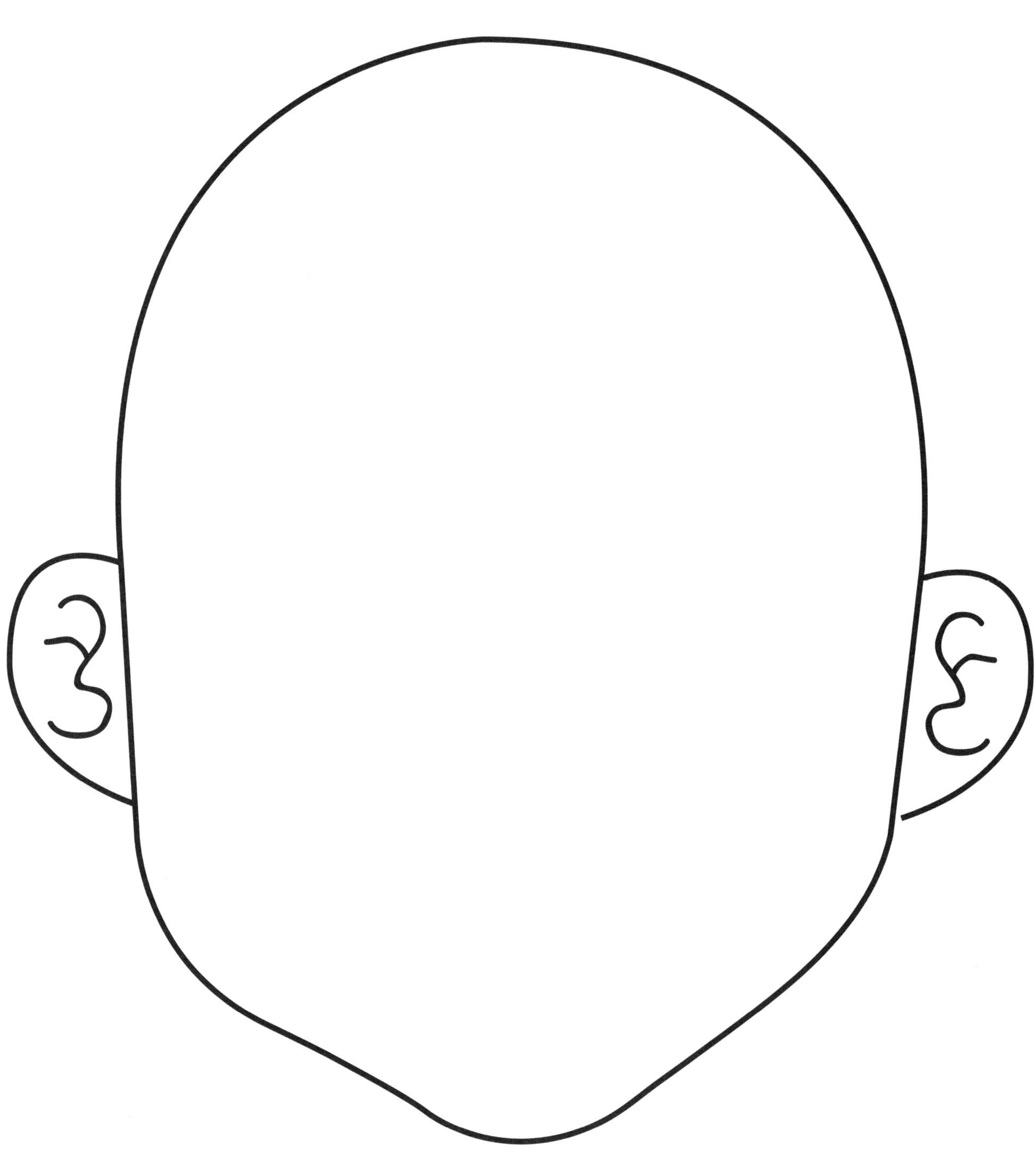

 

# Praise the Lord

## Memory Verse

*Praise him, sun and moon! Praise him, all you twinkling stars!* Psalm 148:3

## Book of Psalms

The Book of Psalms is a collection of verses or hymns in the Bible. They're all about worshiping God! Even the stars, moon, and sun worship God.

# Ordered to Worship an Idol

## Memory Verse

*We will never serve your gods or worship the gold statue you have set up.* Daniel 3:18

## Refusing to Worship a False God (Daniel 3:1–18)

King Nebuchadnezzar of Babylon had his servants make a huge golden idol. It was ninety feet tall! The king called all of his people together to tell them whoever did not worship the idol would be thrown into a blazing furnace. The king heard that Shadrach, Meshach, and Abednego were not obeying his law. They worshiped the one true God!

# Thrown into a Furnace

## Memory Verse

*If we are thrown into the blazing furnace, the God whom we serve is able to save us.* Daniel 3:17

## Saved from the Fire (Daniel 3:19–30)

Shadrach, Meshach, and Abednego refused to bow down to the king's golden idol. The king had them thrown into a blazing furnace. The furnace was so hot that the soldiers who threw in the three men were killed by the blaze. But as the king looked at the furnace, he saw four men walking in it, not three! He called for Shadrach, Meshach, and Abednego to come out of the blazing furnace. They came out completely unharmed by the fire. The Lord was the fourth person in the furnace, and he protected them. The king praised God because no other god had this kind of power.

Draw fire in the furnace and smoke coming out of the chimneys.

# Daniel Prays

## Memory Verse

*The officials went together to Daniel's house and found him praying and asking for God's help.* Daniel 6:11

## Daniel Would Not Stop (Daniel 6:1–11)

Daniel prayed a lot. Three times a day, he would go home and pray to God. Some men who did not like Daniel talked the king into making a new law. This law said that anyone caught praying to God would be thrown into a den of lions. But this new law did not stop Daniel from praying. Color the picture.

# Daniel in the Lions' Den

## Memory Verse

*Not a scratch was found on [Daniel], for he had trusted in his God.* Daniel 6:23

## Daniel Was Saved (Daniel 6)

The king made a new law that declared everyone had to worship him. Daniel disobeyed. He prayed to God. As punishment, Daniel was thrown in the lion's den. God was faithful to Daniel and sent an angel to shut the lions' mouths. Draw closed mouths and whiskers on the lions. Color the picture.

# Jonah Prayed and God Answered

## Memory Verse

*I cried out to the LORD in my great trouble, and he answered me.* Jonah 2:2

## God Heard Jonah's Prayers (Jonah 2)

God did not let Jonah drown. Instead, God sent a big fish to swallow Jonah. Jonah prayed to God while he was in the belly of the fish. After three days, God answered Jonah's prayers. The big fish spat Jonah onto dry land. Write your own prayer on the fish below. Color the fish.

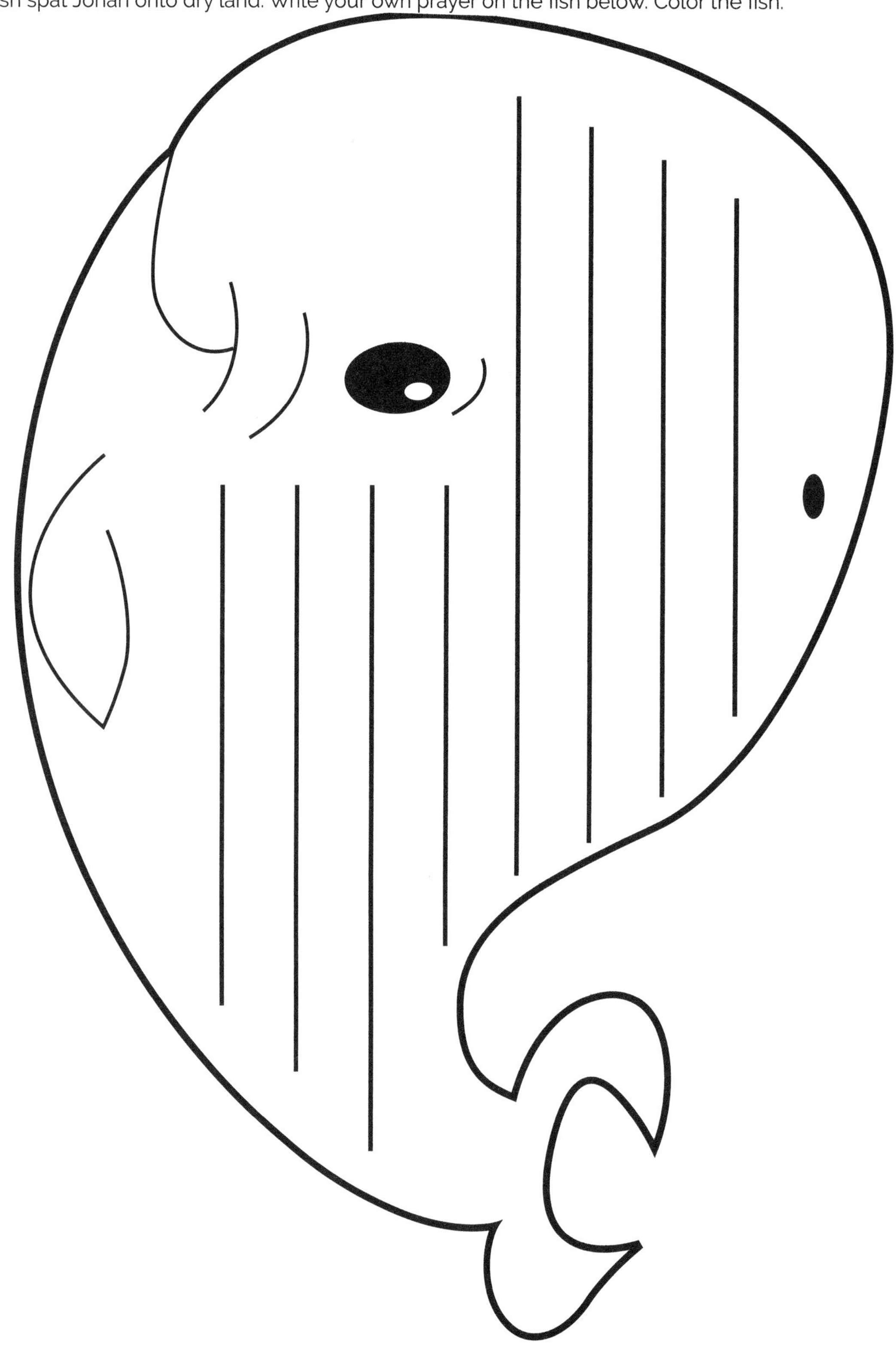

# Jonah on the Beach

## Memory Verse

*I cried out to the LORD in my great trouble, and he answered me.* Jonah 2:10

## Jonah Is Safe (Jonah 2:1–10)

Jonah was in the fish's belly for three days and three nights. He prayed to God to help him, and God did! The great fish spat Jonah onto the shore and Jonah was safe.

Draw the great fish swimming away in the sea. Color the picture.

# Zechariah and Elizabeth

## Memory Verse

*How kind the Lord is!* **Luke 1:25**

## A Son to Prepare the People (Luke 1:5–25)

Zechariah was a priest who worked in the temple serving God. He and his wife, Elizabeth, were very old and had no children. One day an angel told Zechariah that they would have a son who would serve God in a special way. This son, who would be known as John the Baptist, prepared people for the coming of Jesus. Color the picture.

# A Simple Couple

## Memory Verse

*Joseph [was] the husband of Mary. Mary gave birth to Jesus, who is called the Messiah.* Matthew 1:16

## Joseph and Mary

God chose Mary and Joseph to be the mother and earthly father of his Son, Jesus. They were poor, ordinary people. Joseph was a carpenter, and Mary was a young bride, but God used them in his plan to send a Savior to the world.

Draw some carpenter tools on the table, such as a hammer and a saw. Color the picture.

# An Angel Appeared

## Memory Verse

*Mary responded, "I am the Lord's servant. May everything you have said about me come true."* Luke 1:38

## An Angel Told Good News (Luke 1:26–38)

Mary was a young woman who loved God very much. One night, an angel came to visit her. The angel had wonderful news for Mary. God had chosen her to be the mother of his Son. "You will . . . give birth to a son, and you are to call him Jesus," the angel said (Luke 1:31). God was pleased that Mary would be the mother of his Son, Jesus. Mary thanked God for choosing her.

Connect the dots in the picture below to see who brought Mary good news. Color the picture.

# A Special Angel

## Memory Verse

*He will be very great and will be called the Son of the Most High.* Luke 1:32

## An Angel Delivered Good News (Luke 1:26–38; Matthew 1:18–25)

One day, God asked his special messenger angel to tell people that his Son, Jesus, was coming to Earth to be the Savior of the world! Imagine how happy the angel was to announce that wonderful news. Imagine how surprised Mary and Joseph were to see the angel.

You can make an angel that looks like a mosaic. Follow the numbers to see which colors to use.

# An Angel Visited Mary

## Memory Verse

*The Lord is with you.* Luke 1:28

## Important News (Luke 1:26–38)

God sent the angel Gabriel to tell Mary some very important news: she would be the mother of Jesus, God's own Son. Mary was frightened at first by this unusual visitor. But Mary trusted God and accepted the task of mothering Jesus. Color the picture.

# Journey to Bethlehem

## Memory Verse

*Because Joseph was a descendant of King David, he had to go to Bethlehem in Judea, David's ancient home.* Luke 2:4

## Mary and Joseph (Luke 2:1–5)

The Roman government made a law that all Jews had to pay taxes in the towns from which their families came. Mary and Joseph's families were from Bethlehem, about seventy miles from Nazareth, where they were living. So Mary and Joseph began their journey to Bethlehem. Color the picture.

# Jesus' Birthday

## Memory Verse

*The virgin will conceive a child! She will give birth to a son.* Matthew 1:23

## Celebrating Jesus' Birth (Luke 2:1–7)

Christmas is the day we celebrate Jesus' birthday. We don't know if Bible families celebrated birthdays like we do today, but it must have been a joy for Mary and Joseph as they watched their baby, Jesus, grow up. Color the picture.

# Jesus Is the Light of the World

## Memory Verse

*The one who is the true light, who gives light to everyone, was coming into the world.* John 1:9

## Eternal Light (John 1:1–18)

The Jewish people waited many years for the promised Savior. They expected a great king who would rule over them, but instead God sent a baby to an ordinary Jewish girl in a dark, dingy stable. That baby is the eternal Son of God who gave light and life to the world then and today. This was God's plan. Color the picture.

# The Mother of Jesus

## Memory Verse

*The time came for the baby to be born.* Luke 2:6

## Mary (Luke 2:1–7)

You may have seen drawings of Mary, Jesus' mother, on Christmas cards. Mary was a real person who had to go through some hard times. She always followed God and did what he asked her to do. Mary gave birth to baby Jesus in a place where animals were kept because there was nowhere else to stay.

Color the picture of Joseph, Mary, and baby Jesus.

# Jesus Arrived

## Memory Verse

*She wrapped him snugly in strips of cloth and laid him in a manger, because there was no lodging available for them.* Luke 2:7

## Humble Birthplace (Luke 2:1–7)

Jesus was born in a place where animals slept and ate. He slept in a manger, where cows kept their food. He was raised by Mary and Joseph, who were ordinary people. God planned Jesus' humble birth. God wanted everyone, rich or poor, to feel invited and welcome to become part of his family. Color the picture.

# Part of God's Plan

## Memory Verse

*She gave birth to her firstborn son.* Luke 2:7

## Unusual Birthplace (Luke 2:1–7)

Jesus was placed in a manger after he was born. A manger is a feeding box for animals. Because there was no room at the inn, Mary and Joseph had to stay in a place where animals were kept. This would have been a dark, dirty, and smelly place to spend the night. Certainly not a place to give birth to a baby! But it was all part of God's plan.

# **An Angel** Visits the Shepherds

## Memory Verse

*An angel of the Lord appeared among them, and the radiance of the Lord's glory surrounded them.* Luke 2:9

## The Sky Lit Up (Luke 2:8–20)

It was nighttime on the hillsides of Bethlehem. Some shepherds were in the fields watching their sheep when an angel suddenly appeared. The whole sky lit up, and the shepherds were terrified! The angel told them not to be afraid because he had good news about the birth of Jesus. Before long, the sky was filled with many angels praising God. Color the picture.

# Shepherds Hurried to Bethlehem

## Memory Verse

*The shepherds said to each other, "Let's go to Bethlehem!"* Luke 2:15

## A Special Visit (Luke 2:8–20)

An angel announced to the shepherds that Jesus was born in Bethlehem. The Hebrew people had waited a long time for this Messiah. The angel invited the shepherds to see the baby Jesus. The shepherds did not hesitate to leave their flocks and hurry off to Bethlehem. Color the picture.

# A Stable Instead of a Hospital

## Memory Verse

*They hurried to the village and found Mary and Joseph. And there was the baby, lying in the manger.* Luke 2:16

## A Humble Birthplace (Luke 2:16–17)

When the shepherds found Jesus, there were no clean beds or even nurses or doctors. The Jewish people were expecting a Savior, but they thought that he would be born in a palace, not a place where animals lived. But God had his own plans. The important thing is that Jesus was born to save us from our sins. Color the picture.

# Mary Was Thoughtful and Comforting

## Memory Verse

*Mary kept all these things in her heart and thought about them often.* Luke 2:19

## A Good Mother (Luke 2:4–19)

Mary was Jesus' mother. God chose her to be Jesus' mother because she was faithful to God. Right after Jesus was born, the shepherds came to visit Jesus. They told Mary and Joseph how the angels appeared to them in the fields and told them where to find the newborn baby Jesus. Mary felt happy that she was chosen to take care of Jesus, keeping him safe and loved. Color the picture.

# The Magi Followed the Star

## Memory Verse

*Wise men from eastern lands arrived in Jerusalem, asking, "Where is the newborn king of the Jews? We saw his star as it rose, and we have come to worship him."* Matthew 2:1–2

## Seeking the New King (Matthew 2:1–2)

Wise men, sometimes called Magi, followed the star to find Jesus. These Magi were wise men who studied stars and realized that a new king had been born for the Jews. They possibly traveled thousands of miles to Jerusalem. Color the picture.

# The Visit of the Magi

## Memory Verse

*They entered the house and saw the child with his mother, Mary, and they bowed down and worshiped him.* Matthew 2:11

## Finding Jesus (Matthew 2:1–12)

King Herod sent the Magi to Bethlehem because this was the prophesied birthplace of the Messiah. When the Magi arrived, they caused a stir among the people by asking for the newborn king of the Jews. Then the Magi found Jesus. They worshiped Jesus and gave him three kinds of gifts.

Decorate the boxes that contained the three kinds of gifts and draw bricks on the house. Color the picture.

# People Celebrated Jesus' Birth

## Memory Verse

*[Simeon] took the child in his arms and praised God.* Luke 2:28

## Anna and Simeon Worshiped Jesus (Luke 2:21–39)

When Jesus was a baby, Mary and Joseph took him to the temple to dedicate him to the Lord. While the family was there, two elderly people, Simeon and Anna, blessed and worshiped baby Jesus. Anna gave thanks to God. Simeon took Jesus into his arms and thanked God for Jesus.

Using the color key, color the picture of Mary, Joseph, Simeon, and Anna with baby Jesus. Your picture will look like the colorful stained-glass windows that are in some churches.

1 = white
2 = tan
3 = blue
4 = dark green
5 = purple
6 = yellow
7 = pink
8 = light green
9 = brown
10 = red

# Baby Jesus

## Memory Verse

*I have seen your salvation.* Luke 2:30

## Simeon and Anna (Luke 2:21–40)

When Jesus was a baby, Mary and Joseph took him to the temple. They gave an offering to God for Jesus. An man named Simeon was at the temple. God made Simeon know that this baby was God's Son. Simeon took Jesus in his arms and thanked God for sending the Savior. Simeon was so thankful for seeing the Savior, he sang a song of thanks. Anna was a woman who lived at the temple. She saw Simeon holding Jesus. She thanked God for the baby, too.

Color the picture of Simeon and Anna.

# Jesus and His Father

## Memory Verse

*He will be called a Nazarene.* Matthew 2:23

## Living in Nazareth (Matthew 2:23)

Jesus grew up in a small town called Nazareth where he helped his earthly father, Joseph, a carpenter. Jesus was called the carpenter's son. He learned from his father how to make things out of wood. Color the picture.

# Jesus Grew

## Memory Verse

*[Jesus] was filled with wisdom, and God's favor was on him.* Luke 2:40

## Jesus Helped Joseph (Luke 2:40,51–52)

Jesus was once a child just as you are. The Bible says that Jesus obeyed God and his parents. You can obey God and your parents, too. Jesus probably helped his mother, Mary, clean up their house. Jesus probably helped Joseph work in his carpentry shop.

# Jesus as a Child

## Memory Verse

*When Jesus was twelve years old, they attended the festival.* Luke 2:42

## Jesus and Me (Luke 2:41–52)

Jesus was once a child like you. He went to celebrations with his family and friends. He ran in the fresh air. Jesus learned to take turns and share. Jesus did many of the same things you do. His mother watched Jesus grow and learn about his world.

Color the picture of Jesus playing with friends. Your picture will remind you that Jesus was once a child, just like you.

# Jesus Obeyed His Parents

## Memory Verse

*Obey your father's commands, and don't neglect your mother's instruction.* Proverbs 6:20

## Found in the Temple (Luke 2:41–52)

Every year, Jewish families would go to Jerusalem for the Feast of Passover. When Jesus was twelve years old, he stayed behind after his parents left to go home to Nazareth. When they discovered he was missing, Mary and Joseph went back to Jerusalem and found Jesus in the temple, listening and asking questions. Even though Jesus knew that he was the Son of God, he obeyed his mother and earthly father and went home with them. Color the picture.

# Mary and Jesus Went to Market

## Memory Verse

*Jesus grew in wisdom and in stature and in favor with God and all the people.* Luke 2:52

## A Good Childhood (Luke 2:51–52)

When God chose Mary to be Jesus' mother, he knew she would give Jesus the proper care and teaching that Jesus needed. Although Jesus was God's Son, he had a normal childhood with a loving and caring mother just like any other boy of his day.

# Jesus Is the Lamb of God

## Memory Verse

*Look! The Lamb of God who takes away the sin of the world!* John 1:29

## John the Baptist (John 1:27–34)

John the Baptist preached to huge crowds as he prepared the people for Jesus' ministry. He said in John 1:27 that he was not even good enough to untie Jesus' sandals because he knew that Jesus, the Lamb of God, would have to die to save us and that we could not save ourselves.

Draw the sandals on Jesus' feet. Color the picture.

# Jesus Pleased God

## Memory Verse

*You are my dearly loved Son, and you bring me great joy.* Luke 3:22

## John Baptized Jesus (Matthew 3:13–17)

John baptized new believers in the Jordan River. One day, Jesus went to see John. "Baptize Me," Jesus said. John baptized Jesus. When Jesus came up out of the water, the clouds opened up and God spoke from heaven. God said, "You are my dearly loved Son, and you bring me great joy."

Color the picture below according to the color code. Then draw and color the sun.

# Jesus Walked along the Sea of Galilee

## Memory Verse

*Jesus was walking along the shore of the Sea of Galilee.* Matthew 4:18

## Walking along the Shore (Matthew 4:18–22)

When Jesus began his ministry, he moved to Capernaum, a big town beside the Sea of Galilee. The Sea of Galilee is a large lake. Many men earned a living from fishing there. Walking along the sea was an ideal place to find fishermen, and that's exactly what Jesus did.

# Fishers of People

## Memory Verse

*Come, follow me, and I will show you how to fish for people!* Matthew 4:19

## Follow Jesus (Matthew 4:18–22)

As Jesus was walking along the Sea of Galilee, he saw Simon Peter and his brother Andrew fishing with nets. Jesus called them to follow him. He said that he would make them fishers of men. So the brothers left their nets, boats, and fish to follow Jesus. By being fishers of men, they would now help to tell others about Jesus.

Draw lots of fish in the net. Color the picture.

# Follow Me

## Memory Verse

*Come, follow me, and I will show you how to fish for people!* Mark 1:17

## Jesus Found His First Disciples (Mark 1:14–20)

As Jesus walked beside the Sea of Galilee, He saw Simon and his brother Andrew casting a net into the lake. They were fishermen. "Come, follow me," Jesus said. They left their nets and followed him. He saw James and his brother John in a boat, preparing their nets. Without delay he called them, and they left their boat and followed him. Color the picture.

# Jesus Made Fishermen His Disciples

## Memory Verse

*[The fishermen] left their nets at once and followed him.* Mark 1:18

## Seeking Fishermen (Mark 1:14–20)

Jesus wanted ordinary men to be his followers. Many of these men were fishermen. They fished with big nets and pulled the nets into their boats. They knew the importance of working hard. Jesus wanted men whom he could teach because these men would continue to spread the gospel after Jesus went to heaven. Color the picture.

# Peter Went Fishing

## Memory Verse

*Their nets were so full of fish they began to tear!* Luke 5:6

## Colorful Catch (Luke 5:1–11)

While Jesus was on Earth, he did many miracles. These miracles showed the people God's power, and that Jesus really was God's Son. Jesus' miracles also showed how much God loves all people. Once, Peter had fished all night but had not caught any fish. Jesus told him to try again. This time so many fish came into Peter's net that the net broke and the fish filled two boats!

Color all the B's brown. Color all the R's red. Color all the Y's yellow.
Color all the G's blue. Draw fishermen in the boat.

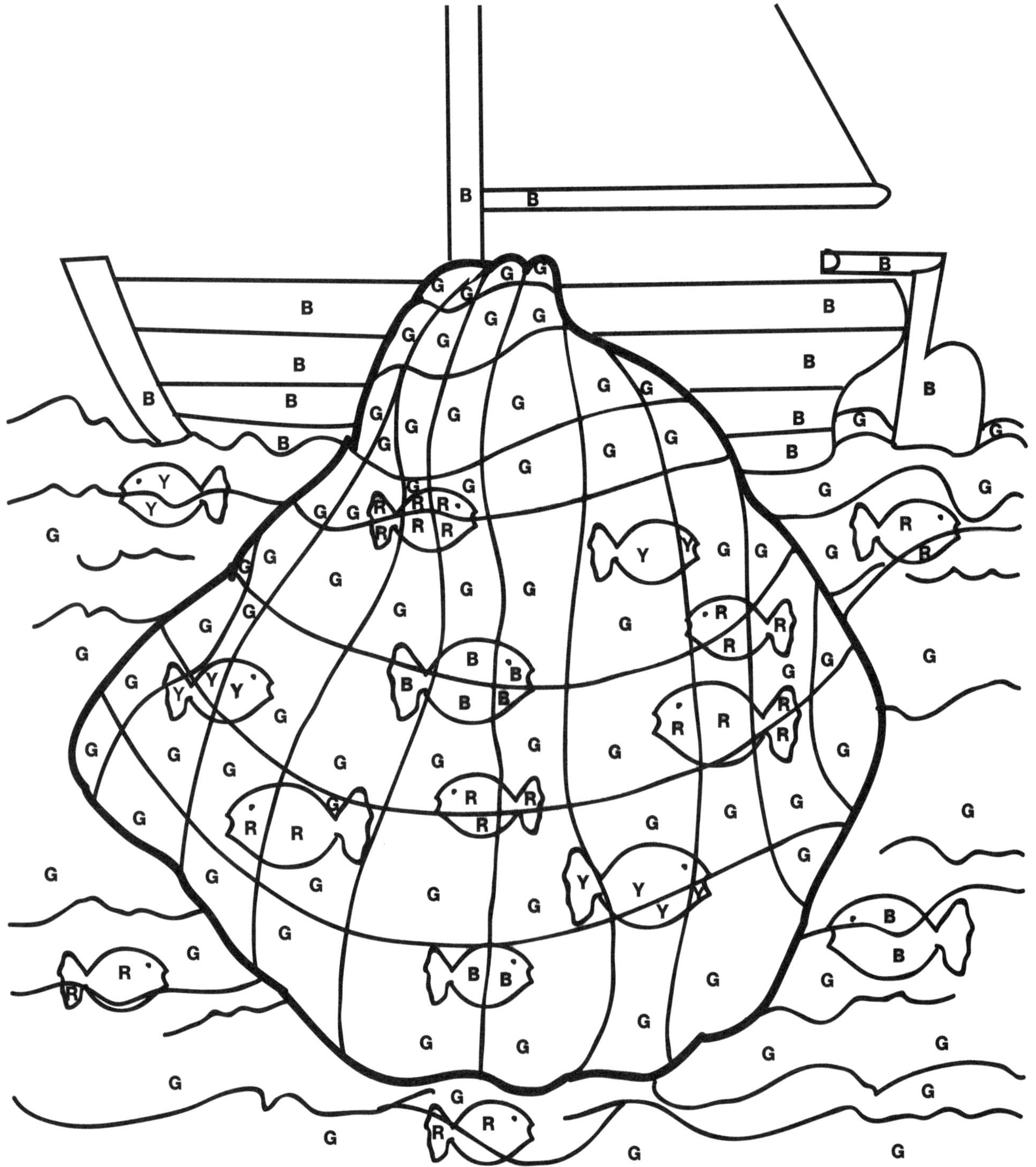

 

# A Net of Fish

## Memory Verse

*Soon both boats were filled with fish.* Luke 5:7

## A Full Net (Luke 5:1–11)

Peter and Andrew were brothers and fishing partners. One day while they were repairing their fishing nets, Jesus told them to go out into the deep part of the water and let down their nets. Peter and Andrew had fished all night in that same lake without catching even one fish. But they obeyed Jesus. Their nets were so full they couldn't hold all the fish!

Color the fish. Draw a net around them by using a black crayon to draw crisscross lines.

# Follow Jesus

## Memory Verse

*They left everything and followed Jesus.* Luke 5:11

## Following Our Leader (Luke 5:1–11)

Peter and Andrew were fishermen. When Jesus told them to follow him, they obeyed.. We can follow Jesus by coming to Sunday school, worshiping at church and at home, praying, and in many other ways.

Color the picture of Jesus, our leader.

## Memory Verse

*The touch of [Jesus'] hand healed every one.* Luke 4:40

# Jesus Healed Many (Luke 4:38–41)

People learned that Jesus performed miracles and healed the sick. They brought to Jesus people who had all kinds of sickness, and laying his hands on each one, he healed them. Demons came out of some people, shouting, "You are the Son of God!" But he would not allow them to speak, because they knew he was the Messiah. Color the picture.

# The Wedding Helper

## Memory Verse

*This miraculous sign at Cana in Galilee was the first time Jesus revealed his glory.* John 2:11

## Miracle at a Wedding (John 2:1–11)

One day Jesus, his disciples and his mother attended a wedding. All of them had fun until the wine ran out. Jesus' mother knew he could help, and he did. After Jesus told the servants to fill the water jugs with water, a miracle happened. The water became wine! The wedding guests were very happy.

Follow the numbers to color the picture.

# A Woman at the Well

## Memory Verse

*A Samaritan woman came to draw water, and Jesus said to her, "Please give me a drink."* John 4:7

## Special Water (John 4:5–15)

While Jesus was traveling through the country of Samaria, he stopped at a well to rest. In Bible times, people got their drinking water from a well, and they had to carry it home in large jugs. Around noon, a woman came to the well to get water. Jesus asked her to give him a drink. She was surprised that he spoke to her because men did not talk to women in public in those days, especially not a Samaritan. Jews and Samaritans were enemies. Jesus told the Samaritan woman that he could give her a special kind of water and she would never be thirsty again. The woman was curious. She wanted to learn more about this water. Color the picture.

# Living Water

## Memory Verse

*Give me this water! Then I'll never be thirsty again.* John 4:15

## Never Be Thirsty Again (John 4:10–26)

Jesus offered the woman at the well living water so that she would never be thirsty again. She didn't understand at first, but Jesus was talking about himself. Jesus satisfies us the same way that water does when we are thirsty. Jesus also told her about the bad things she had done in her life, and she was amazed that he knew. She finally realized that Jesus was the Messiah. She left her jar at the well and ran into the town to tell others that she had just met Jesus, the Savior.

Draw a jug of water on the well. Color the picture.

# Jesus Healed a Sick Boy

## Memory Verse

*The man believed what Jesus said.* John 4:50

## A Happy Boy (John 4:46–54)

A very important man came to see Jesus. "Please, Jesus," the man said, "Come quickly! My boy is very sick. Please come and make him well again." Jesus gently said, "You can go home again. Your son lives!" The man went home and found his boy was well, just as Jesus said!

Color the dotted sections to find the happy boy Jesus made well.

# Jesus Healed a Sick Man

## Memory Verse

*Stand up, pick up your mat, and walk!* John 5:8

## He Got Up and Walked Home (John 5:1–9)

There was a special pool of water in Jerusalem. Many sick people lay near the water. They wanted to be healed from their sicknesses, but many of them did not have anyone to help them get into the water. One man had been sick for thirty-eight years! Jesus saw the man and felt sorry for him. The man said he wanted to be healed, so Jesus made him well. The man got up and walked home! Color the picture.

# Nothing without God

## Memory Verse

*Whatever the Father does, the Son also does.* John 5:19

## Some People Don't Believe Jesus (John 5:16–23)

Jesus is the Son of God. But when he walked this earth, many people did not believe he was God. The religious teachers didn't like Jesus healing the sick and crippled. They were mad when Jesus raised people from the dead. They didn't want him saying that he was God's Son. But who else can do such wonderful things? Only God's Son could do miracles.

Jesus said he is not complete without God. Draw the right side of Jesus to match the left to make the picture of him complete. Color the picture.

# Friends Carried a Man on a Cot

## Memory Verse

*The house where he was staying was so packed with visitors that there was no more room, even outside the door.* Mark 2:2

## A Large Crowd (Mark 2:1–4)

Jesus went from town to town preaching and healing people. One day, when he was preaching at a home in Capernaum, there was such a huge crowd that it was hard to get near Jesus. Four men who heard of Jesus' healing power came carrying a crippled friend on a mat. When the friends saw the crowd, they did not get discouraged, but instead looked for another way to get to Jesus Color the picture..

# Finding a Way

## Memory Verse

*They dug a hole through the roof above his head. Then they lowered the man on his mat, right down in front of Jesus.* Mark 2:4

## A Sick Man was Lowered Through the Roof (Mark 2:4–12)

The four friends of the crippled man had faith that Jesus could heal him. Since they could not get through the crowd, they decided to take him to the roof. The friends made a hole in the roof and lowered the crippled man to Jesus. The crippled man was healed because of their faith in Jesus.

Draw ropes coming from the hole in the roof to the handles on the mat. Color the picture.

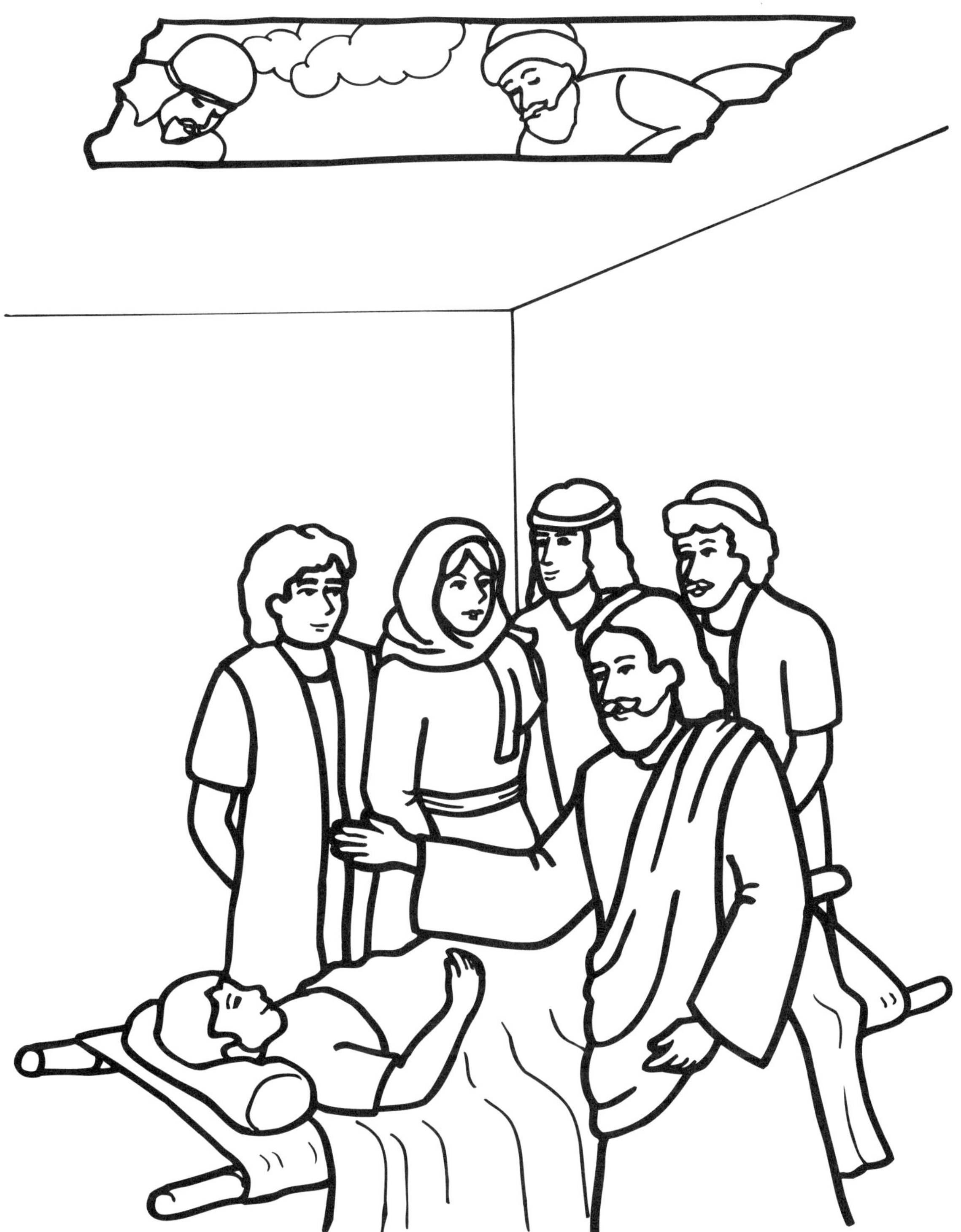

# Jesus Prayed

## Memory Verse

*Jesus went up on a mountain to pray, and he prayed to God all night.* Luke 6:12

## Praying to God (Luke 6:12–16)

Jesus knew the power of praying to God. One day, he went up a mountainside and prayed to his Father in heaven all night long. He had an important decision to make. He had to choose his twelve apostles. When you have an important decision to make, you should pray, too. Color the picture.

# Prayer

## Memory Verse

*When you pray, go away by yourself, shut the door behind you, and pray to your Father in private.* Matthew 6:6

## Pray to Your Father (Matthew 6:5–15)

Jesus taught people about prayer. He said when you pray, go into your room, close the door, and pray to your Father, who is unseen. Then your Father, who sees what is done in secret, will reward you Color the picture. .

# Do Not Worry

## Memory Verse

*Why worry about your clothing? Look at the lilies of the field and how they grow. They don't work or make their clothing.* Matthew 6:28

## God Cares for You (Matthew 6:25–34)

Jesus says it is wrong to worry because God even takes care of little birds and flowers. Jesus wants us to know that we should not worry about anything. God takes care of the birds, the flowers, and everything in his world. Also, he cares for us! Who can take better care of us than God? Nobody!

Color the picture of the bird and flowers.

# The House on a Rock

## Memory Verse

*Though the rain comes in torrents and the floodwaters rise and the winds beat against that house, it won't collapse because it is built on bedrock.* Matthew 7:25

## The Sturdy House (Matthew 7:24–27)

Jesus told a story about two men who built houses. One man built a house on a rock. The other man built a house on the sand. When it rained, the house built on the rock stayed strong and safe. The house built on the sand fell down. Like the house on the rock, God's love keeps you safe, too.

Color the pictures of tools to remind you of the house built on a rock.

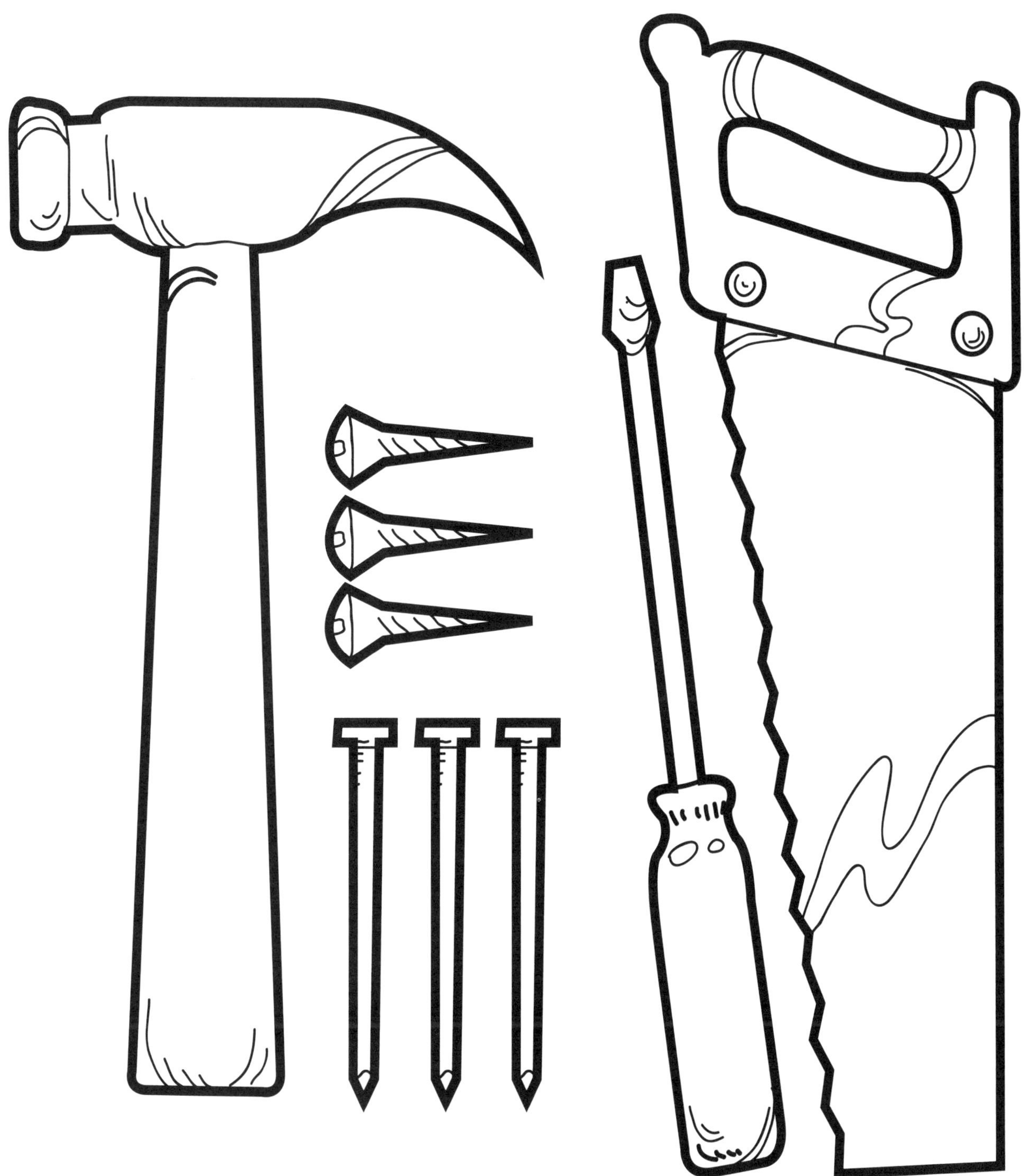

# Foolish Man's House

## Memory Verse

*Anyone who hears my teaching and doesn't obey it is foolish, like a person who builds a house on sand.* Matthew 7:26

## A Poor Foundation (Matthew 7:24–27)

Have you ever played in sand? It might be fun to play in, but you don't want to build your house on it! If we do not do what the Bible says, we are like a foolish person who builds a house on the sand. When we come to church to learn about God but fail to obey him, trouble comes our way just like the storm that crashed the foolish man's house. Draw a stormy sky and rain. Then color the rest of the picture.

# Wise Man's House

## Memory Verse

*Anyone who listens to my teaching and follows it is wise, like a person who builds a house on solid rock.* Matthew 7:24

## Solid Foundation (Matthew 7:24–25)

When your house has a strong and solid foundation, you do not have to be afraid that it will fall apart during a storm. It will keep you safe. Jesus told about the wise man who built his house on rock. When the storm came, he was safe. The things we learn from the Bible will protect us, too, if we are wise and practice them.

Draw windows in the house and storm clouds in the sky. Color the picture.

# Parable of the Soils

## Memory Verse

*A farmer went out to plant some seed.* Mark 4:3

## Hear the Word and Accept It (Mark 4:3–20)

Jesus told a story about a farmer who planted some seeds. The seeds that fell along the pathway were eaten by birds. The seeds that fell on the rocky soil died because there was not enough soil for them to grow. The seeds that fell among the thorns and weeds grew for a little while but were soon choked out and died. The seeds that fell on the good, rich soil grew up strong and provided the farmer with lots of food at harvest. Color the picture.

# The Waves Obeyed Jesus

## Memory Verse

*When he gives a command, even the wind and waves obey him!* Luke 8:25

## Jesus Calmed a Storm (Luke 8:23–26)

Jesus and his disciples were in a boat on a lake when a furious storm arose. The disciples were scared, but Jesus was sleeping. They woke Jesus. He ordered the wind and the waves to be calm, and the storm ended. Jesus is God's Son—he can do anything! Draw a stormy sky. Color the picture.

# The Wind Obeyed Jesus

## Memory Verse

*Even the wind and waves obey him!* Mark 4:41

## In Control (Mark 4:35–41)

Jesus' disciples found themselves in the middle of a terrible storm. Jesus was asleep in the boat. The disciples were afraid and woke up Jesus. Jesus told the wind and the waves to be still. Immediately all was quiet. Color the picture.

# Jesus Asleep on the Boat

## Memory Verse

*As they sailed across, Jesus settled down for a nap. But soon a fierce storm came down on the lake.* Luke 8:23

## Jesus Was Not Afraid (Luke 8:22–23)

One day, Jesus and his disciples got into a boat and headed for the other side of the Sea of Galilee. Jesus fell asleep as they sailed. Suddenly, a violent storm arose and water gushed into the boat. The disciples were in danger of drowning. Color the picture.

# Jesus Calmed the Sea

## Memory Verse

*When Jesus woke up, he rebuked the wind and the raging waves. Suddenly the storm stopped and all was calm.* Luke 8:24

## All Became Calm (Luke 8:22–25)

The disciples were afraid. They panicked as the storm raged around them. Jesus was sleeping. Finally, the disciples called out to him to save them. Jesus stood up and immediately calmed the sea by his command. The disciples were amazed that all of nature obeyed Jesus.

Draw the calm sea, the shining sun, and clouds in the sky. Color the picture.

# Just Believe

## Memory Verse

*Don't be afraid. Just have faith.* Mark 5:36

## Jairus's Daughter (Mark 5:21–24; 35–43)

As Jairus and Jesus approached the house, they were told that Jairus's little girl had already died. They were too late. Jairus was so sad. But Jesus had other plans. He loved the little girl and Jairus very much. Because of his love and great power, he was able to heal the little girl.

Color the picture of Jesus, Jairus, and the happy little girl.

# A Dying Little Girl

## Memory Verse

*A man named Jairus . . . came and fell at Jesus' feet, pleading with him to come home with him. His only daughter . . . was dying.* Luke 8:41–42

## Jairus Begged Jesus for Help (Luke 8:40–42, 49)

As Jesus traveled from town to town, many people crowded around him, wanting to be healed. One day, a man named Jairus came to Jesus and begged him to come to his house. He said his only daughter, who was twelve years old, was dying. Jairus knew Jesus could heal her. He loved her very much. But as Jesus was traveling to Jairus' house, someone told him that Jairus' daughter had died already. It was too late—or so they thought! Color the picture.

# A Little Girl Is Alive

## Memory Verse

*Her life returned, and she immediately stood up!* Luke 8:55

## Saved from Death (Luke 8:49–56)

Jesus went immediately to Jairus's house, even though the little girl had just died. Her family was crying because they were very sad. Jesus told them not to worry. He said she was not dead, only asleep. They laughed at him because they knew she was not asleep. Jesus went into her room, took her by the hand, and told her to get up. And she did just that! Jesus brought her back to life! Jairus and the girl's mother were amazed at the miracle, and they believed in Jesus.

Draw a pillow at the end of the little girl's bed. Color the picture.

# Touched by Jesus

## Memory Verse

*Just have faith, and she will be healed.* Luke 8:50

## Made Whole Again (Luke 8:40–42,49–56)

There was once a man named Jairus. He had a beautiful twelve-year-old daughter. One day she became very sick and was about to die. Jairus heard that Jesus was in his town. He knew that if Jesus touched his little girl she would be made well. He ran and brought Jesus to his home. But it was too late. Everyone was crying because the little girl had died. Jesus said, "Do not cry. The girl is only sleeping." Everyone laughed. They knew she was dead. Jesus took the girl's hand. Suddenly, she opened her eyes and stood up! Everyone was so excited!

Draw the missing half of the girl, then color the picture.

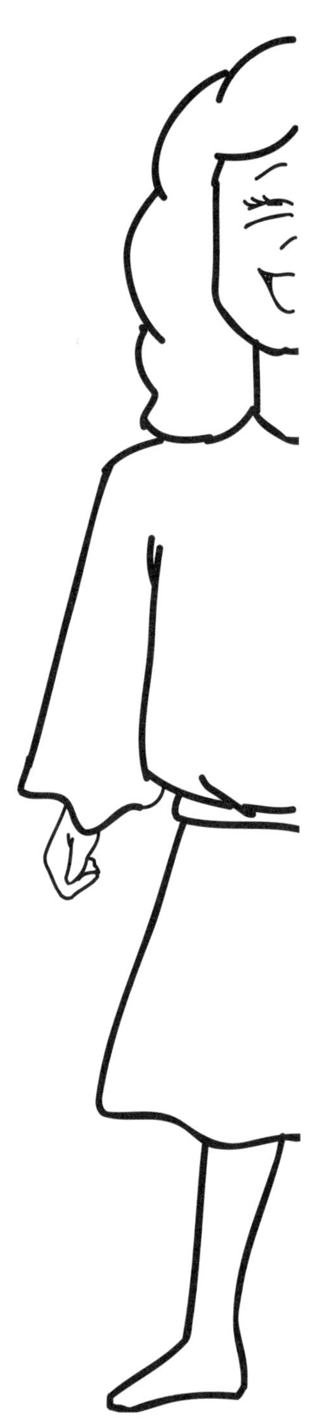

# Teaching the Multitude

## Memory Verse

*He welcomed [the crowds] and taught them about the Kingdom of God, and he healed those who were sick.* Luke 9:11

## Listening to Jesus (Luke 9:10–17)

It was difficult for Jesus and his disciples to get away by themselves without interruptions. One day, over 5,000 people followed Jesus because they had heard about his miraculous healing power. He could have sent them all away, but instead he gladly welcomed them. Jesus loved and cared for them. Color the picture.

# Feeding the Many

## Memory Verse

*There's a young boy here with five barley loaves and two fish. But what good is that with this huge crowd?* John 6:8–9

## Five Loaves and Two Fish (John 6:5–14)

It was getting late in the day as Jesus preached and healed. The disciples became worried about what the people would eat since there were so many. They wanted to send them all home, but Jesus had another plan. He took a boy's five bread loaves and two fish and miraculously fed over 5,000 people!

Draw the five bread loaves and the two fish in the boy's basket. Color the picture.

# A Boy Shared His Lunch

## Memory Verse

*I am the bread of life. Whoever comes to me will never be hungry again.* John 6:35

## Sharing with Others (John 6:5–14; 25–40)

People flocked to Jesus wherever he was. Word of his miracles spread quickly. One day, Jesus spoke all day to a very large crowd. He knew that it was getting late and thought they must be hungry. A young boy, who had brought some food, was willing to share. Because the boy was obedient to Jesus, great things were able to happen. Through his miraculous powers, Jesus was able to take that small little lunch and feed the many people who were there to listen to him. Draw crowds of people behind Jesus and the boy. Color the picture.

# I Can See

## Memory Verse

*"It was not because of his sins or his parents' sins," Jesus answered. "This happened so the power of God could be seen in him."* *John 9:3*

## Jesus Performed Miracles (John 9:1–12)

Jesus walked around and talked to people about God's kingdom. He healed many people. One day, Jesus came upon a blind man. Some people thought he was blind because he or his parents had sinned. Jesus mixed dirt with his spit and put it on the man's eyes. When the man washed the mud away, he could see! Jesus told the people that no one had sinned; the man was blind to show God's power Color the picture.

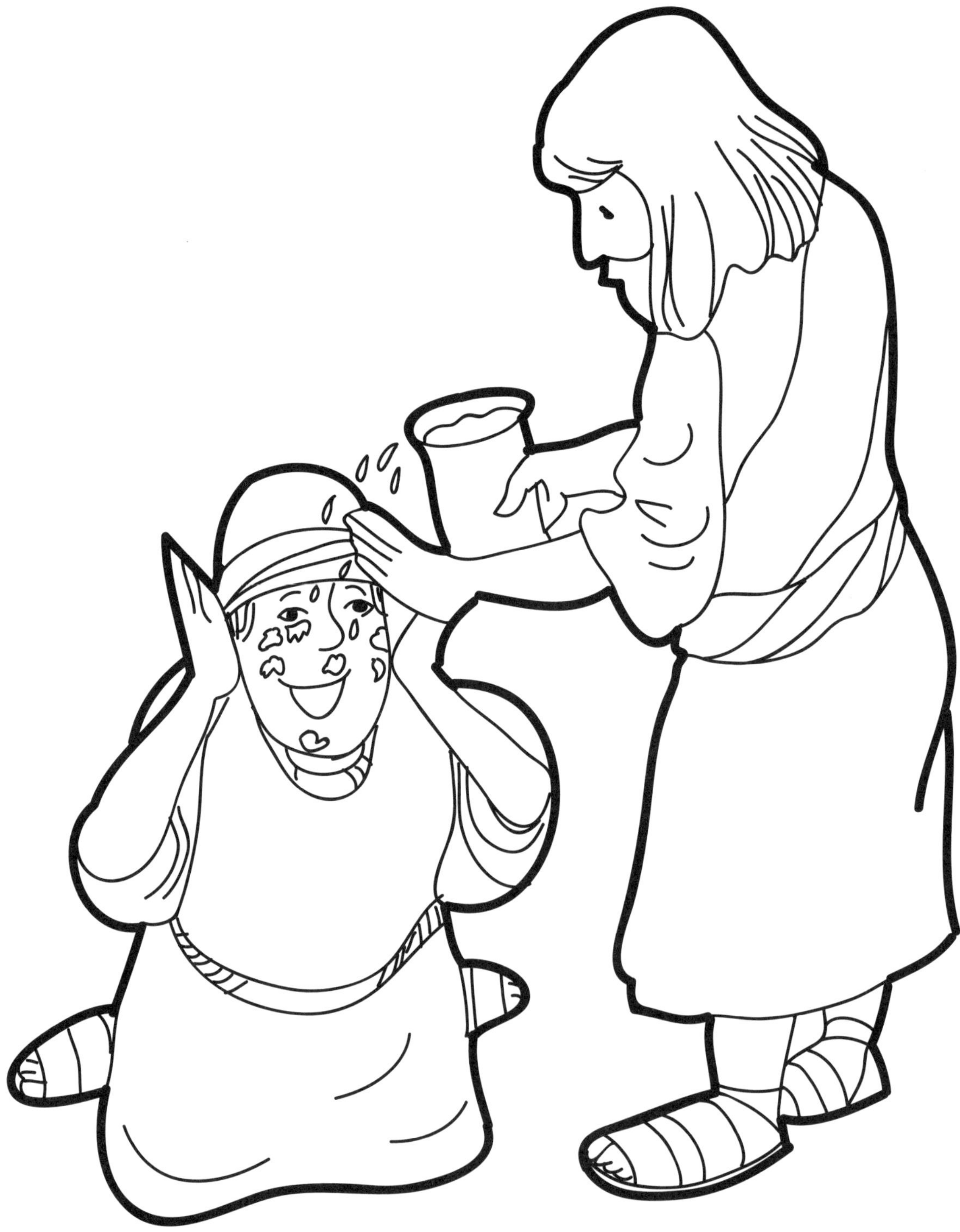

# A Surprise Coin

## Memory Verse

*Open the mouth of the first fish you catch, and you will find a large silver coin.* Matthew 17:27

## Money in a Fish (Matthew 17:24–27)

Jesus told Peter to go fishing. He said, "Open the mouth of the first fish you catch, and you will find a large silver coin." Peter obeyed Jesus. When he looked inside the mouth of his first fish, he was surprised to find money. There was enough money to pay Jesus' tax and Peter's tax, too! Jesus made sure Peter had the money they needed for taxes.

Color your fish and draw a coin in its mouth.

# Little Ones

## Memory Verse

*Don't look down on any of these little ones. For I tell you that in heaven their angels are always in the presence of my heavenly Father.* Matthew 18:10

## Jesus with Children (Matthew 18:1–5)

Jesus cares for children as much as for adults. He tells us not to look down on children because God loves them, too. The Bible says that guardian angels are assigned to watch over his children. These angels are always near God, who is in heaven. Isn't it wonderful that God protects us with guardian angels? Color the picture.

# Helping Others

## Memory Verse

*The Samaritan soothed his wounds.* Luke 10:34

## A Good Man (Luke 10:25–37)

Jesus told a story about a good man who lived in Samaria. The good Samaritan stopped to help a hurt man beside the road. He wrapped the hurt man in bandages and found him a place to stay. Jesus wants us to be kind and help others like the Good Samaritan did. Color the picture.

# The Good Samaritan

## Memory Verse

*When [the Samaritan] saw the man, he felt compassion for him.* Luke 10:33

## Who Is My Neighbor? (Luke 10:30–37)

When Jesus taught his disciples the parable of the good Samaritan, Jesus was teaching them about loving their neighbors. In the parable, two men saw a beaten man and ignored him. Then, the Good Samaritan saw that the man needed help and felt sorry for him. He took the man to an inn and cared for him until he was well. Our neighbors are not just people who live next to us. Everyone is our neighbor! Color the picture.

# Be the Samaritan

## Memory Verse

*When God our Savior revealed his kindness and love, he saved us . . . because of his mercy.* Titus 3:4–5

## It's Always Good to Help (Luke 10:30–37)

Read the parable of the good Samaritan. First a priest, and then a Temple assistant, saw the beaten man. They didn't want to be bothered with him, so they ignored him by traveling on the other side of the road. But Jesus wants us to be like the Good Samaritan who showed his love toward this man. Have you ever helped someone who needed your help?

In the picture, a boy has fallen on the sidewalk. Would you be a Good Samaritan like the girl and help him pick up his books? Draw books on the sidewalk and tears on the boy's face. Color the picture.

# Be Kind

## Memory Verse

*Be kind to each other.* Ephesians 4:32

## Remember to be Kind to Others (Luke 10:30–37)

The good Samaritan story teaches us to be kind and help others. There are many ways to be kind. At home, you can pick up your toys, help set the table, and be gentle with your pets. At church, you can take turns, share toys, and listen when the teacher is talking. Jesus is happy when we are kind, like the Good Samaritan who stopped to help the hurt man.

Color this picture, and it will remind you to be kind to others.

# Jesus Visited Mary and Martha

## Memory Verse

*A woman named Martha welcomed [Jesus] into her home.* Luke 10:38

## Welcoming Jesus (Luke 10:38)

Mary and Martha were sisters who both loved Jesus very much. They also had a brother named Lazarus. Jesus often visited them at their home. They were wonderful hosts, and they welcomed Jesus with open arms. Color the picture.

# Our Heavenly Father

## Memory Verse

*For everyone who asks, receives. Everyone who seeks, finds. And to everyone who knocks, the door will be opened.* Luke 11:10

## Heavenly Gifts (Luke 11:5–13)

One day, Jesus was teaching some people about God. Jesus told them that God was their Father in heaven. If you asked your dad for some bread, would he give you a rock instead? If you asked for some fish to eat, would he give you a snake? Of course not. Jesus told the people that they could ask for anything, and God would hear their prayers. God is your heavenly Father who loves and protects you.

Our Father in heaven gives us all good things. How many things can you thank God for in this picture? Color the picture.

# God Knows All

## Memory Verse

*Don't be afraid; you are more valuable to God than a whole flock of sparrows.* Luke 12:7

## No One Is Forgotten (Luke 12:6–7)

Jesus spoke to his disciples as a large crowd was gathering to see him. He was telling them how God knows all that we say and all that we do, and none of us is forgotten. "What is the price of five sparrows—two copper coins? Yet God does not forget a single one of them. And the very hairs on your head are all numbered. So don't be afraid; you are more valuable to God than a whole flock of sparrows." Color the picture.

# The Shepherd Protects His Flock

## Memory Verse

*I am the good shepherd. The good shepherd sacrifices his life for the sheep.* John 10:11

## The Good Shepherd (John 10:1–16)

There were many sheep in the land where Jesus lived. Shepherds took care of the sheep. The shepherds kept the sheep safe and fed them. Jesus is the Good Shepherd. He cares for us. Jesus helps keep us safe and provides us with the food we eat.

Use a brown crayon to draw the shepherd's staff. Color the picture.

# The Lost Sheep

## Memory Verse

*Rejoice with me because I have found my lost sheep.* Luke 15:6

## Finding the Stray (Luke 15:1–7; John 10:27)

Jesus told a story about a shepherd who cared for his sheep. When one sheep got lost, the shepherd looked and looked for the sheep. When he found the sheep, the shepherd carried the sheep home and took care of it. The shepherd was very happy he found the sheep. We should try to follow Jesus, our Shepherd.

Color the sheep that are listening to the shepherd and following him. Put an X on the sheep that are not listening and not following the shepherd. Color the picture.

# Lost and Found

## Memory Verse

*If a man has a hundred sheep and one of them gets lost, what will he do? Won't he leave the ninety-nine others in the wilderness and go to search for the one that is lost until he finds it?* Luke 15:4

## The Shepherd Finds His Sheep (Luke 15:3–7)

Jesus told a story about a shepherd who looked and looked for a sheep that was lost. The shepherd was very happy when he found the sheep. He carried the sheep home and took care of it. Jesus loves us and is taking care of us as the good shepherd took care of his lost sheep.

Can you find some lost sheep in the picture? Color them black. Color the picture.

# Sheep Know the Shepherd's Voice

## Memory Verse

*My sheep listen to my voice; I know them, and they follow me.* John 10:27

## Lost Sheep Found (Luke 15:4–7)

When the shepherd finally found his lost sheep, he picked it up, put it on his shoulders, and took it home. He then called his friends and neighbors together to celebrate. The shepherd knew that the lost sheep was disobedient in wandering off from the flock, but he loved it very much and was happy to find it. God loves us, too, even when we disobey him. He is always willing to forgive us when we ask. Draw a sheep in the shepherd's arms. Color the picture.

# Jesus Told a Parable

## Memory Verse

*The LORD is my shepherd; I have all that I need.* Psalm 23:1

## Sinners are the Lost Sheep (Luke 15:1–7)

Some men were angry because Jesus let sinners gather around him to listen. So Jesus told the parable of the Lost Sheep. Jesus' followers are sheep, and he is our Shepherd. Color the picture.

# Parable of the Lost Coin

## Memory Verse

*Suppose a woman has ten silver coins and loses one. Won't she light a lamp and sweep the entire house and search carefully until she finds it?* Luke 15:8

## Every Person Is Precious (Luke 15:8–10)

Did you ever lose something that you really treasured? What did you do about it? Jesus told about a woman who treasured ten silver coins and lost one of them. She did not give up searching through her house until she found it. Every person is precious to God, just like the coin was precious to the woman. God is sad when we are lost and not obeying him, but he rejoices when we are sorry and try to do better.

Draw the woman's lost coin on the floor. Color the picture.

# Repent

## Memory Verse

*There is joy in the presence of God's angels when even one sinner repents.* Luke 15:10

## Angels in Heaven Rejoicing (Luke 15:8–10)

In the same way that the woman rejoiced with her friends over finding her treasured coin, the angels in heaven rejoice when we repent and accept Jesus as Lord. *To repent* means to be sorry for your sins. Jesus' mission on Earth was to bring lost sinners to salvation through him.

Draw a happy face on the angel. Color the picture.

# Parable of the Lost Son

## Memory Verse

*Filled with love and compassion, [the father] ran to his son, embraced him, and kissed him.* Luke 15:20

## Forgiveness (Luke 15:11–32)

Jesus told a story about a boy who ran away from home. When the boy had no more money, he got a job feeding pigs. He was so hungry, he wanted to eat the pigs' food.. The boy was sorry for what he had done and he decided to go home. His father forgave him and had a big party to welcome him back. Just like the boy's father, Jesus will forgive us when we are sorry that we have done wrong things.

The boy probably had nice clothes when he left home. On the picture, draw how the boy looked when he was hungry and feeding the pigs. You can draw some of the pigs, too. How do you think the boy looked after his father forgave him? Color the picture.

# The Lost Son & the Pigs

## Memory Verse

*The young man became so hungry that even the pods he was feeding the pigs looked good to him. But no one gave him anything.* Luke 15:16

## Ending Up in a Pig Pen (Luke 15:11–19)

Jesus tells a parable about a son who wasted his inheritance money on having a good time. When his money was gone, he had to get a job feeding pigs. He had nothing to eat. It did not take the son long to realize he had made a mistake. Sometimes we, too, end up in a "pig pen" before we realize how wrong we have been. When we disobey God over and over again, our only way out is to ask him for forgiveness. God is always faithful when we turn back to him. Color the picture.

# The Lost Son Returned

## Memory Verse

*This son of mine was dead and has now returned to life. He was lost, but now he is found.* Luke 15:24

## Forgive Others (Luke 15:20–32)

The lost son's father was so excited to see him return home that he gave him a hug, a kiss, a robe, a ring, sandals, and a party to celebrate! What a homecoming! Only one person was not happy to see him return—his older brother. He always had obeyed his father and worked very hard for him. The father freely forgave the lost son because he loved him. The older brother refused to forgive him and could not understand the mercy his father showed. Don't be like the brother. Forgive others because God forgives them, and he also forgives us.

Draw a ring on the lost son's finger and sandals on his feet. Color the picture.

# Martha Ran to Meet Jesus

## Memory Verse

*Lord, if only you had been here, my brother would not have died.* John 11:21

## Martha and Jesus (John 11:1–37)

Mary and Martha sent word to Jesus that their brother Lazarus was very sick and needed healing. Jesus, who loved Lazarus, did not rush to heal him, but instead waited two more days before he went. Martha ran to meet Jesus when she heard he was finally coming, but it was too late because Lazarus was already dead. Mary and Martha could not understand why Jesus was not there when they needed him. Color the picture.

# Believe in Jesus

## Memory Verse

*I am the resurrection and the life.* John 11:25

## Jesus Is Life (John 11:1–44)

Mary and Martha were sad because their brother, Lazarus, had died. Martha greeted Jesus when she heard he was nearing her village. Jesus said to her, "I am the resurrection and the life . . . Whoever lives and believes in me will never die." Mary and Martha believed in Jesus. Jesus went to the tomb where Lazarus was buried and called out to him. Lazarus came out, alive. All who believe in Jesus will have everlasting life.

Use the color key to color the picture of Jesus.

1 = brown

2 = tan

3 = blue

4 = green

5 = red

6 = yellow

7 = purple

8 = orange

# Lazarus Lived

## Memory Verse

*Everyone who lives in me and believes in me will never ever die.* John 11:26

## Jesus Raised Lazarus from the Dead (John 11:1–44)

Mary, Martha, and Lazarus were brother and sisters. They were also Jesus' friends. When Lazarus became very sick, Mary and Martha asked Jesus to come quickly. They knew he had the power to heal people. But Jesus stayed where he was for two more days. Lazarus died! When Jesus arrived at their house, everyone was sad. Jesus went to the tomb where Lazarus was buried and said, "Lazarus, come out." Lazarus walked out of the tomb. He was alive!

Color the picture of Lazarus walking out of the tomb. Color the picture.

# Jesus Brought Lazarus Back to Life

## Memory Verse

*Didn't I tell you that you would see God's glory if you believe?* John 11:40

## Lazarus Made Alive Again (John 11:34–44)

Mary and Martha took Jesus to the tomb where Lazarus' body was placed. Jesus had the huge stone in front of the tomb moved away. After praying to God, He called in a loud voice, "Lazarus, come out!" To everyone's amazement, Lazarus came out alive! Many of the Jews with Mary and Martha put their faith in Jesus after seeing this.

Draw the huge stone that was moved away from the tomb. Color the picture.

# One Came Back

## Memory Verse

*One of them . . . came back to Jesus, shouting, "Praise God!"* Luke 17:15

## Jesus Cured Lepers (Luke 17:11–19)

On his way to Jerusalem, Jesus met ten men who had leprosy. They stood at a distance and called out, "Jesus, Master, have mercy on us!" When he saw them, he said, "Go, show yourselves to the priests." As they went, they were cleansed. One of them came back, praising God in a loud voice. He threw himself at Jesus' feet and thanked him. Jesus asked, "Didn't I heal ten men? Where are the other nine?" Then he said to him, "Stand up and go. Your faith has healed you." Color the picture.

# A Blind Man Saw

## Memory Verse

*Jesus said, . . . "Your faith has healed you." Instantly the man could see, and he followed Jesus.* Luke 18:42–43

## The World Is Colorful (Luke 18:35–43)

Jesus was walking to a town. A poor man sat on the side of the road. He was blind. The man heard a crowd coming closer. They were saying that Jesus was coming. The man cried, "Jesus, have mercy on me!" Jesus asked the man what he wanted. "I want to see," said the man. Jesus said, "Then you will see. Your faith has healed you."

The man was so happy. He could see the people. He could see trees. He immediately got up and became one of Jesus' helpers.

Color the picture. Of all the nice things in the picture, what do you think the man was most excited to see?

# Zacchaeus in the Crowd

## Memory Verse

*He tried to get a look at Jesus, but he was too short to see over the crowd.* Luke 19:3

## Zacchaeus Could Not See (Luke 19:1–4)

Everywhere Jesus went, he was followed by crowds of people. When Jesus came to Jericho, a man named Zacchaeus could not see him because he was short. He had heard so much about Jesus, though, that he had to find a way to see him. The crowds would not budge, so he ran ahead and climbed a sycamore tree, where he waited for Jesus to come by. Color the picture.

# Zacchaeus Saw Jesus

## Memory Verse

*He ran ahead and climbed a sycamore-fig tree beside the road, for Jesus was going to pass that way.* Luke 19:4

## Zacchaeus Was Forgiven (Luke 19:1–10)

Zacchaeus was a very short man. He wanted to see Jesus, but there were too many people in the way, so he climbed into a tree. Jesus had lunch at Zacchaeus's house. Zacchaeus told Jesus he was sorry for the bad things he had done. Jesus said Zacchaeus was forgiven.

Follow the color key to color the picture of Zacchaeus in the tree.

# Zacchaeus in the Tree

## Memory Verse

*"Zacchaeus!" [Jesus] said. "Quick, come down! I must be a guest in your home today."* Luke 19:5

## Jesus Saw Zacchaeus (Luke 19:1–10)

Jesus was walking with the crowd in Jericho. Zacchaeus was a short man who wanted to see Jesus. He climbed up a sycamore tree to get a better view. Jesus came to the sycamore tree where Zacchaeus was. Jesus looked up and called Zacchaeus to come down at once because he was going to his house that very day! The crowd complained because Zacchaeus was a tax collector who got rich by cheating them. After meeting Jesus, Zacchaeus' heart changed.

Draw Zacchaeus' money bag tied around his waist. Color the picture.

# Jesus Blessed the Children

## Memory Verse

*Anyone who doesn't receive the Kingdom of God like a child will never enter it.* Mark 10:15

## Jesus Loved Children (Mark 10:13–16)

Jesus loves children. When he lived on Earth, he was happy when children came to see him. He held the children in his arms. Maybe he even played games with them!

Now that Jesus is in heaven, he still loves children. He loves you, and he is with you all the time. He is taking care of you and protecting you.

Connect the dashed lines. Draw a picture of yourself next to Jesus. Then color the picture.

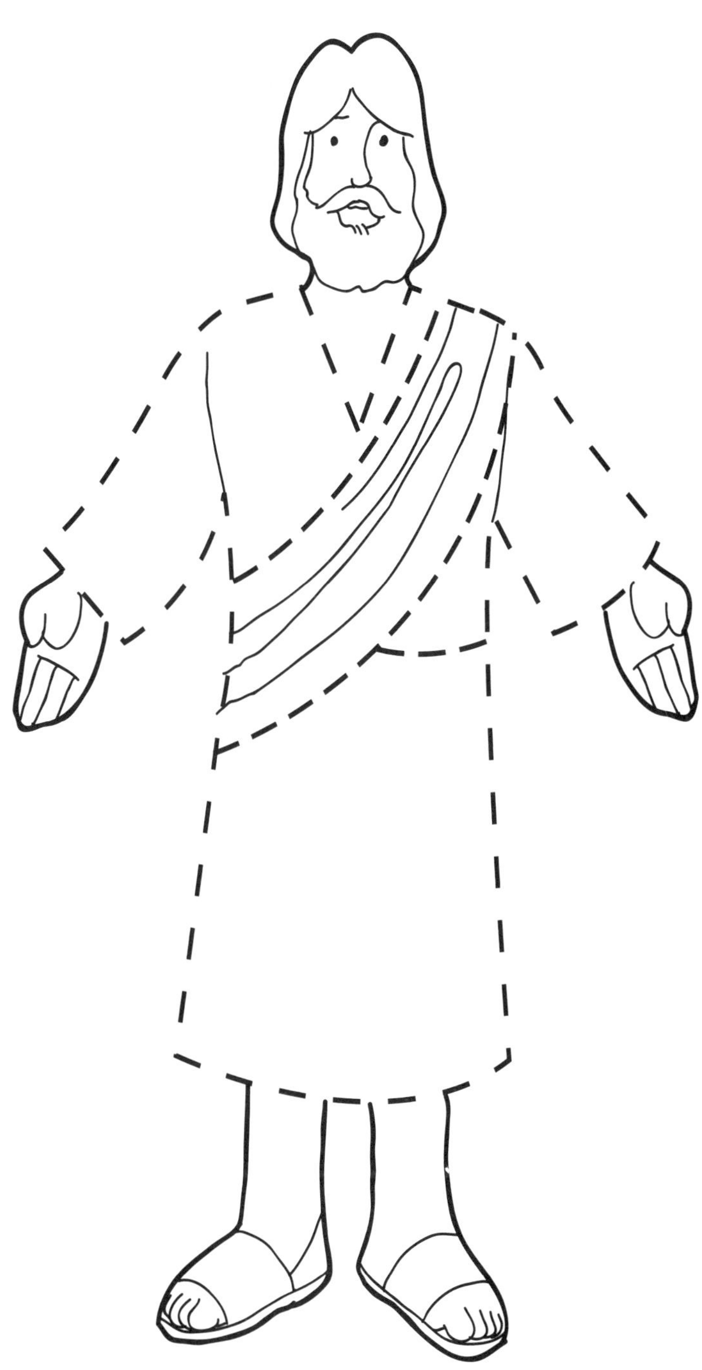

 

# Little Children

## Memory Verse

*Let the children come to me.* Mark 10:14

## Blessed Are the Children (Mark 10:13–16)

One day, some parents brought their children to Jesus. They wanted him to bless them, but his disciples told them to go away. When Jesus saw this, he said to them, "Let the children come to me. Don't stop them! For the Kingdom of God belongs to those who are like these children. I tell you the truth, anyone who doesn't receive the Kingdom of God like a child will never enter it." And he took the children in his arms, placed his hands on them, and blessed them. Draw a child that looks like you! Color the picture.

# The Rich Young Ruler's Treasure

## Memory Verse

*If you want to be perfect, go and sell all your possessions and give your money to the poor, and you will have treasure in heaven.* Matthew 19:21

## Riches Mean Nothing (Matthew 19:16–22)

One day, a very rich young man came up to Jesus and asked him what he must do to go to heaven some day. Jesus told him he must obey the commandments. The young man replied that he had been doing that since he was a boy. Then Jesus told him to sell everything that he owned, give the money to poor people, and follow him. This young man had lots of money, and he was quite happy living his life in luxury. He was very sad at hearing this because his heart was not with Jesus. His heart belonged to the things he owned. He just couldn't give them up, so he walked away from Jesus. Color the picture.

# A Family Jesus Loved

## Memory Verse

*A dinner was prepared in Jesus' honor.* John 12:2

## A Special Visitor (John 12:1–3)

Jesus had no home of his own. Mary, Martha, and Lazarus were a special family who welcomed him whenever he came to visit. Martha cooked Jesus' favorite foods. Mary sat at Jesus' feet and listened to him. Lazarus talked with Jesus. All of them were very excited when Jesus came to visit.

Connect the broken lines to show Jesus at his friends' door. Color the picture.

# Mary's Gift for Jesus

## Memory Verse

*Mary took a twelve-ounce jar of expensive perfume . . .*
*and she anointed Jesus' feet with it.* John 12:3

## Mary Poured Perfume on Jesus' Feet (John 12:1–3)

Jesus came to visit his friends Mary, Martha, and Lazarus. Mary poured sweet-smelling perfume on Jesus' feet and dried his feet with her hair. The whole house smelled wonderful from her gift to Jesus. Draw oil coming out of Mary's vase and color the picture.

# Honor Jesus

## Memory Verse

*Take delight in honoring each other.* Romans 12:10

## A Dinner Was Given to Honor Jesus (John 12:1–8)

Mary and Martha planned a dinner to Jesus' honor. They remembered that he had raised Lazarus from the dead. Martha prepared special food and served them. While Jesus was reclining, Mary took a jar of very expensive perfume and poured it on Jesus' feet. Then she used her hair to wipe them. Mary showed honor to Jesus with this special gift.

Color the picture of Mary pouring perfume on Jesus' feet.

# Jesus Entered Jerusalem

## Memory Verse

*Blessings on the one who comes in the name of the LORD!* Matthew 21:9

## Triumphant Arrival (Matthew 21:1–11)

Jesus came to Jerusalem riding on a donkey as people cheered. Those in the large crowd placed their cloaks in the road ahead of Jesus and spread a layer of palm branches in the path. Color the picture.

# The Triumphal Entry

## Memory Verse

*Many in the crowd spread their garments on the road ahead of him, and others spread leafy branches they had cut in the fields.* Mark 11:8

## Palm Celebration (Mark 11:1–10)

When the great Feast of Passover was about to begin, Jesus rode into Jerusalem on a donkey. People heard that he was coming so they took palm branches and shouted, "Blessings on the one who comes in the name of the LORD!" They wanted Jesus to be the king and ruler of their land. They did not understand that he wanted to be the King and Ruler of their hearts. Color the picture.

# A Crowd Greeted Jesus

## Memory Verse

*"Praise God . . . Hail to the King of Israel!* John 12:13

## Blessed Is the King (John 12:12–18)

A great crowd heard that Jesus was on his way to Jerusalem. They took palm branches and went out to meet him, shouting and praising his name. Color the picture.

# Jesus Forgave Us

## Memory Verse

*This is my blood, which confirms the covenant between God and his people. It is poured out as a sacrifice to forgive the sins of many.* Matthew 26:28

## Body and Blood of Christ (Matthew 26:17–30)

When Jesus was eating the Passover meal, he used the occasion to offer himself as a gift to his disciples. He said the bread was his body and the wine was his blood. The disciples didn't understand yet, but Jesus was preparing them for what was about to take place—his death on a cross. God gave us his Son so that our sins could be forgiven once and for all. It is a gift for everyone who believes in Christ. Color the picture.

# The Upper Room

## Memory Verse

*He will take you upstairs to a large room that is already set up. That is where you should prepare our meal.* Luke 22:12

## Making Preparations (Luke 22:7–13)

When the Feast of Passover arrived, Jesus sent Peter and John to make the preparations. They bought lamb, unleavened bread, wine, and herbs. Jesus told them to go to Jerusalem where a man carrying water would meet them. The man would then take them to a large upstairs room where Jesus and his friends would eat the Passover meal. The disciples did as Jesus said and prepared the meal.

Draw a window in the upstairs room. Color the picture.

# The Last Supper

## Memory Verse

*I have been very eager to eat this Passover meal with you before my suffering begins.* Luke 22:15

## The Holy Gathering (Luke 22:14–23)

The Passover meal was the last meal Jesus ate before he was crucified. He and his disciples ate it in the upstairs room that was provided for the occasion. While they ate, Jesus told them that one of them would soon betray him and that one would deny him. This was hard for the disciples to understand, but Jesus knew what the next several hours would bring—his own cruel death on a cross. Color the picture.

# The Garden of Gethsemane

## Memory Verse

*He prayed more fervently, and he was in such agony of spirit that his sweat fell to the ground like great drops of blood.* Luke 22:44

## Praying in the Garden (Luke 22:39–46)

In the evening after the Passover meal, Jesus and his disciples went to the Garden of Gethsemane. Jesus went ahead of the disciples and prayed alone. When he came back to them, he found them sleeping instead of keeping watch and praying. Jesus was suffering terrible agony because he knew what was going to happen to him, yet he was willing to suffer in order to save us from our sins.

Draw trees, flowers, stars, and a moon. Color the picture.

# Peter Denied Knowing Jesus

## Memory Verse

*Again Peter denied it, this time with an oath. "I don't even know the man," he said.* Matthew 26:72

## Denial Three Times (Matthew 26:69–75)

To deny something means to say that it is not true. While the courts questioned Jesus, a servant girl asked Peter if he knew Jesus. Peter pretended not to know who Jesus was. Peter knew exactly who Jesus was, but Peter was scared! He said he did not know Jesus three times. He was very sorry afterward. Color the picture.

# Jesus on Trial

## Memory Verse

*Jesus made no response to any of the charges, much to the governor's surprise.* Matthew 27:14

## Jesus Was Silent (Matthew 27:11–26)

The Jewish leaders wanted Jesus killed. Jesus was brought to Pontius Pilate, the governor, and accused of crimes he never committed. As Pilate questioned Jesus about these crimes, he was silent and did not even try to defend himself. Jesus' only crime was that he claimed to be God. Pilate could find no reason to crucify Jesus, so he let the Jewish leaders decide. Color the picture.

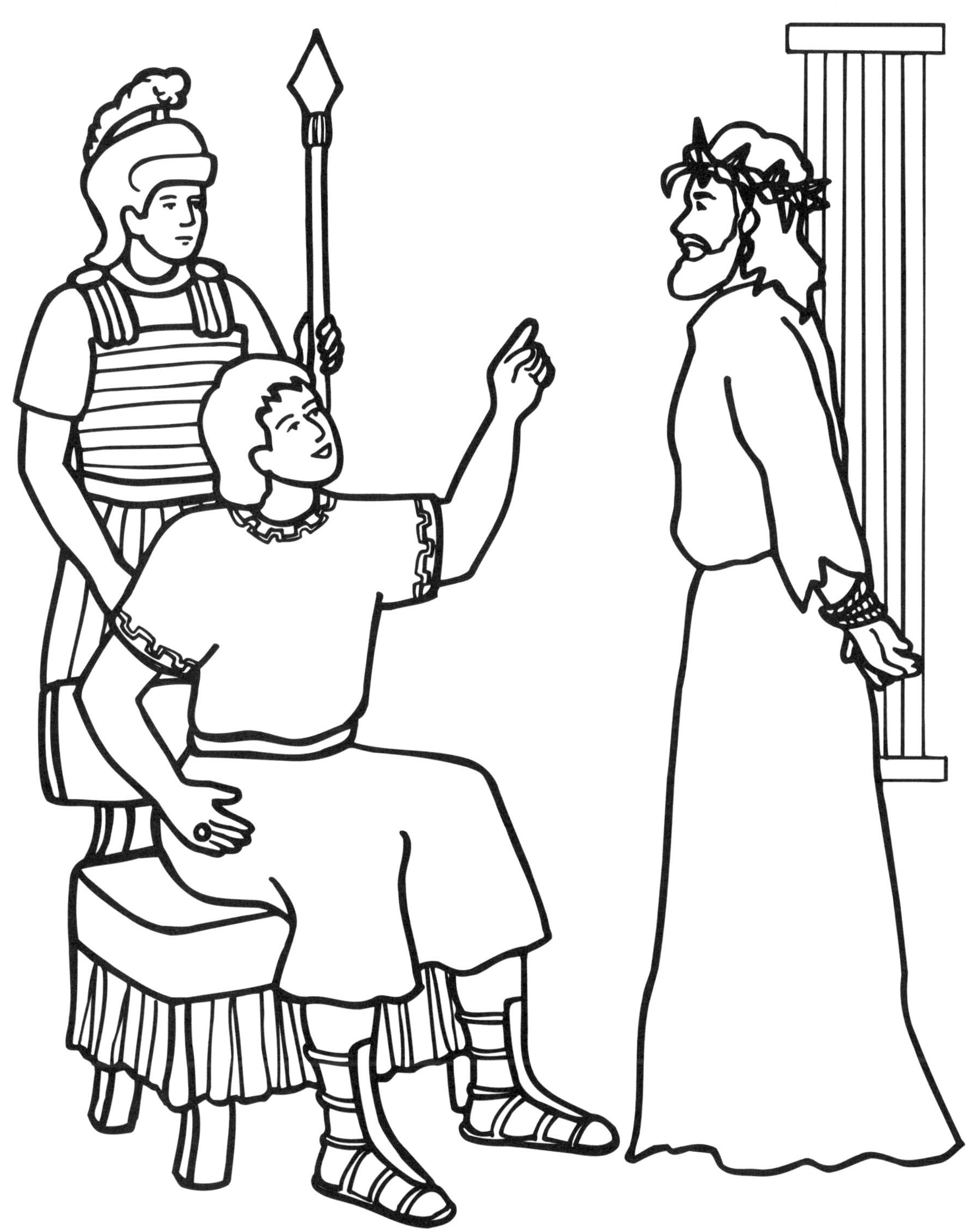

# Jesus Died and Came Alive Again

## Memory Verse

*This man truly was the Son of God!* Matthew 27:54

## The Cross (Matthew 28:1–18)

Jesus loves us and cares for us so much that he died so we can be forgiven for the wrong things we do. Jesus took the punishment we deserved for our sins. When we ask him, Jesus will forgive us for our sins.

To see where Jesus died, color the dotted sections red. Then, color the rest of the sections other colors.

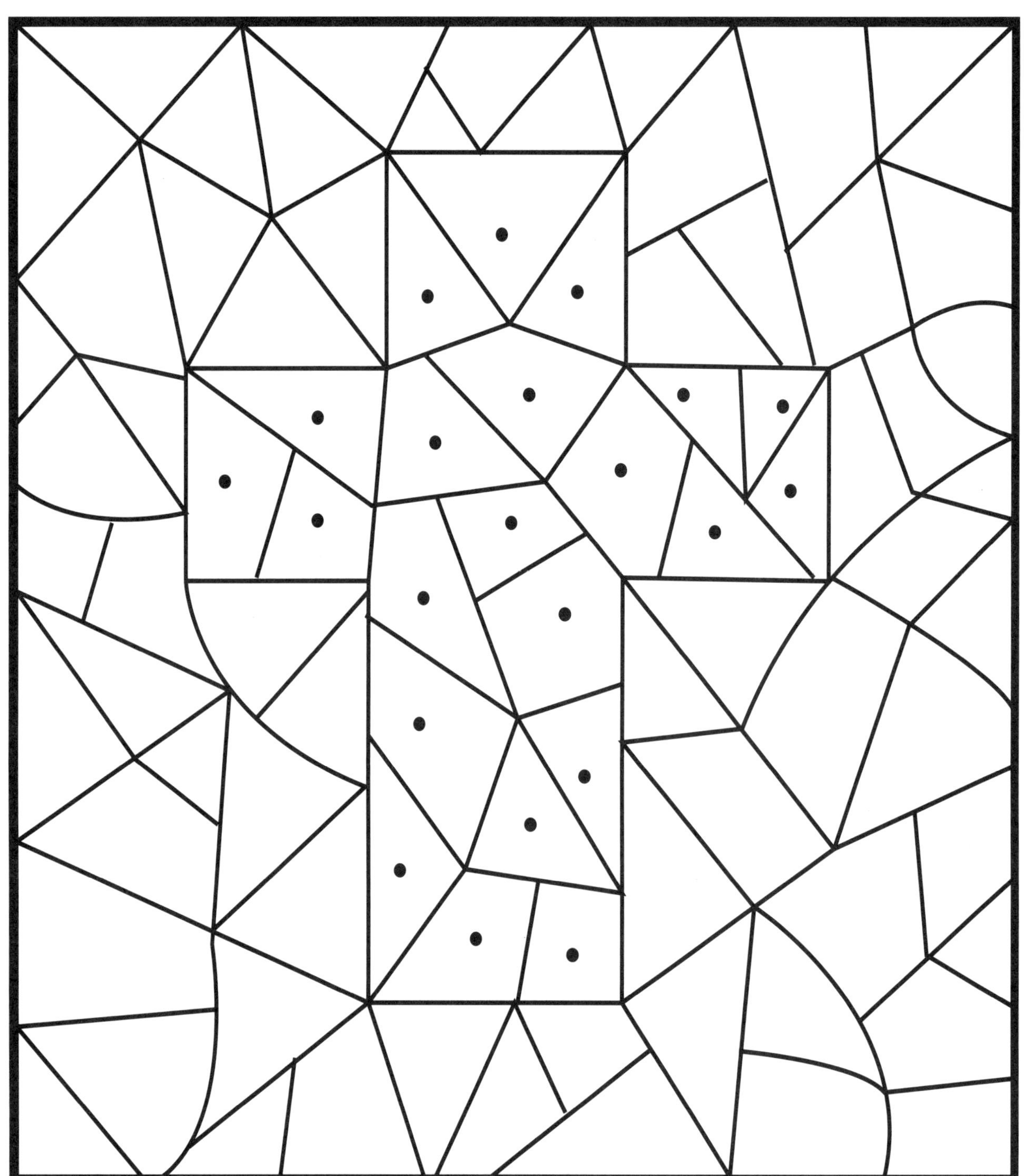

# The Crucifixion

## Memory Verse

*They nailed him to the cross.* John 19:18

## A Sad Event (John 19:16–27; Luke 23:17–43)

Jesus was nailed to a wooden cross for all to see. Many had come to watch the crucifixion, including Jesus' mother. Some who watched yelled insults at him. Some were deeply saddened. There were two criminals nailed to crosses beside Jesus. One criminal mocked him, but the other one recognized him as the Son of God who had done nothing to deserve his punishment. Color the picture.

# The Garden Tomb

## Memory Verse

*He isn't here! He is risen from the dead, just as he said would happen.* Matthew 28:6

## He Has Risen (Matthew 28:1–10)

The greatest news ever proclaimed to the world was the angel's announcement that Jesus had risen from the dead. When the women went to the tomb early in the morning with burial spices, an angel announced, "He is not here. He has risen, just as he said. Come and see the place where he lay."

Draw flowers and a rising sun coming up behind the hills. Color the picture.

# An Angel on the Stone

## Memory Verse

*An angel of the Lord came down from heaven, rolled aside the stone, and sat on it.* Matthew 28:2

## Jesus Lives (Matthew 28:1–15)

After Jesus died on the cross, his body was wrapped in linens and placed in a tomb cut out of rock. The tomb door was sealed shut with a huge stone. Soldiers were posted to keep watch, making sure no one could steal Jesus' body. No one stole his body, yet the tomb became empty. Jesus was alive again! Color the picture.

# Bribed with Money

## Memory Verse

*The LORD detests lying lips, but he delights in those who tell the truth.* Proverbs 12:22

## Paid to Lie (Matthew 28:11–15)

The Jewish leaders did not like the uproar the empty tomb caused among the people. The soldiers who kept watch over the tomb reported what had happened concerning the resurrection. They were given a large amount of money to lie and say that Jesus' disciples came at night to steal his body. A lot of people believed the lies that the soldiers told. Color the picture.

# Jesus and Mary in the Garden

## Memory Verse

*Mary Magdalene found the disciples and told them, "I have seen the Lord!"* John 20:18

## Jesus Appeared (John 20:10–18)

Mary Magdalene came to the tomb early in the morning, only to discover that the stone had been rolled away and that the tomb was empty! She was deeply saddened by the death of her friend Jesus. She wondered who had taken his body. Suddenly, Jesus approached her outside the tomb. She did not even recognize him at first. What joy and happiness she must have felt when she realized Jesus was alive!

Draw flowers and trees in the garden by the tomb. Color the picture.

# Jesus Appeared to His Disciples

## Memory Verse

*[The disciples] were filled with joy when they saw the Lord!* John 20:20

## Happy to See Jesus Alive (John 20:19–30)

After Jesus rose from the dead, he was a real person who walked, talked, ate food, and could be touched. Yet he had the ability to appear to many different people. Jesus first appeared to his disciples in a locked room! They were frightened at first but true joy filled their hearts when they realized that Jesus had risen from the dead, just as he said he would.

Draw happy faces on the two disciples and scars on Jesus' hands. Color the picture.

# Fishing in the Sea of Galilee

## Memory Verse

*Jesus appeared again to the disciples beside the Sea of Galilee.* John 21:1

## Jesus Appeared Again (John 21:1–7)

Jesus appeared again to his disciples by the Sea of Galilee. Some of them decided to go fishing, so they went out in their boat, but that night they caught nothing. Early in the morning, Jesus stood on the shore, but they did not recognize him. He called out to them, "Have you caught any fish?"

"No," they answered. He told them to throw their net out on the right side of the boat. When they did, they were unable to haul the net in because of the large number of fish. Then one of them said to Peter, "It's the Lord!" Color the picture.

# **Breakfast** by the Sea

## Memory Verse

*"Come and have some breakfast!" Jesus said.* John 21:12

## Jesus Had Breakfast Waiting (John 21:1–14)

After Jesus rose from the dead, he appeared to many people. On one occasion, Jesus had breakfast prepared for his disciples on the seashore. They had been fishing in a boat all night without any luck. Jesus called out and told them to throw their net on the right side of their boat. When they did this, they had so many fish that it was difficult to haul them in. The disciples then realized that it was Jesus who was calling to them. They went ashore and had breakfast with him.

Draw the disciples sitting on the shore with Jesus. Color the picture.

# The Ascension

## Memory Verse

*When the Lord Jesus had finished talking with them, he was taken up into heaven.* Mark 16:19

## Jesus Appeared to His Disciples (Mark 16:15–20)

After his resurrection, Jesus appeared to his disciples. He told them to go into the world and teach people about the good news of Jesus Christ, making them disciples and baptizing them. He promised them that he would be with them always. His commands were not just for the disciples but for us, too. Jesus wants us to tell people about him so they will have a chance to be saved.

Draw the clouds around Jesus as he goes up to heaven. Color the picture.

# Jesus Went Home

## Memory Verse

*The disciples went everywhere and preached, and the Lord worked through them, confirming what they said by many miraculous signs.* Mark 16:20

## Up in the Clouds (Mark 16:19–20)

After Jesus died and rose again, he spent time with his friends. They were so happy that he was alive! He walked and talked with them. They listened very carefully to Jesus. Then Jesus lifted his hands. Suddenly, Jesus began to rise into the clouds. Jesus' friends watched. Then they went out and spread the word of Jesus.

Draw some clouds around Jesus. Draw two angels in the sky. Color the picture.

# The Church Began

## Memory Verse

*[Jesus] talked to them about the Kingdom of God.* Acts 1:3

## Encouraged by Jesus' Teachings (Acts 1:1–11)

After Jesus rose from the dead, he came back to Earth and spent forty days with the disciples. When Jesus left the second time, the disciples were brave and ready to tell others about him. They knew he was real and everything he said was true. But before Jesus went up to heaven, he told his disciples to wait in Jerusalem. A special gift from God was coming their way. Color the picture.

# The Holy Spirit Came to a Secret Room

## Memory Verse

*What looked like flames or tongues of fire appeared and settled on each of them.* Acts 2:3

## A Holy Gift (Acts 2:1–5)

God's gift of the Holy Spirit came, just as Jesus promised. A group of Christians were gathered in a house when suddenly a sound like a terrible storm filled the whole place. Then they saw what looked like tongues of fire coming from heaven and landing on each one of them. But, no one was burned. The people realized that God had given them this Spirit and that with the Spirit's help they could begin the job of spreading the good news of Jesus. Draw tongues of fire coming down and landing on the people. Color the picture.

# Peter and John Went to Pray

## Memory Verse

*Peter and John went to the Temple one afternoon to take part in the three o'clock prayer service.* Acts 3:1

## Meeting a Crippled Man (Acts 3:1–10)

Peter and John had a mission: to tell people about Jesus. Sometimes the Holy Spirit gave the apostles power to heal so those people would believe in Jesus. One day as Peter and John were walking to the Temple to pray, they met a man who had never been able to walk. He had to beg for money every day because he could not work to earn money as other people could. Peter and John had no money to give the man, but they had something even better.

Color the picture of Peter and John..

# Peter Healed a Crippled Beggar

## Memory Verse

*He jumped up, stood on his feet, and began to walk!* Acts 3:8

## Jumping for Joy (Acts 3:1–10)

The crippled beggar asked Peter and John for money as they walked by. Instead, God worked through Peter to give the man something even more valuable—the ability to walk! Peter took the man by the hand and the man stood up on both feet. The man was so happy that he went jumping for joy and praising God.

Draw a happy face on the beggar and sandals on his feet. Color the picture.

# Sharing Everything

## Memory Verse

*All the believers were united in heart and mind. . . . They shared everything they had.* Acts 4:32

## Empowered by Jesus (Acts 4:32–35)

With great power, the apostles continued to testify to the resurrection of the Lord Jesus. And God's grace was so powerfully at work in them all that there were no needy people among them. For from time to time, those who owned land or houses sold them, brought the money from the sales, and put it at the apostles' feet, who distributed the money to anyone in need. Color the picture.

# Ananias Lied to God

## Memory Verse

*You must each decide in your heart how much to give. . . .*
*God loves a person who gives cheerfully.* 2 Corinthians 9:7

## Keeping Money for Himself (Acts 5:1–6)

The first Christians shared everything they had with each other. No one needed anything. Some of the Christians even sold their land and gave the money to the apostles. Ananias and Sapphira were a married couple who sold their land and said they would give all the money from it to the apostles. But Ananias decided to keep some of the money for himself. He lied—not only to the apostles but also to God. When Peter asked Ananias about it, Ananias fell down and died. Color the picture.

# Sapphira Lied to God

## Memory Verse

*Be a good worker, one who does not need to be ashamed and who correctly explains the word of truth.* 2 Timothy 2:15

## Keeping Money from the Land (Acts 5:7–11)

Sapphira went to see the apostles. She didn't know what had happened to Ananias. The apostles asked if the amount of money they received for the land was correct. Sapphira knew in her heart it was not, but she lied and said yes anyway. Just like her husband, who also lied, she died because of her sin.

Draw a money bag in Sapphira's hand. Color the picture.

# Saul Obeyed God

## Memory Verse

*Saul! Saul! Why are you persecuting me?* Acts 9:4

## Saul Changed His Ways (Acts 9:1–9)

Saul hated anyone who followed Jesus. He did not want people to obey Jesus. He even killed some people. One day, Jesus said to Saul, "Stop hurting me." Saul then knew that Jesus was God's Son. He stopped hurting Jesus' friends. From that time on, Saul obeyed God.

Color the picture by following the color key.

1=Brown

2=Green

3=Yellow

4=Blue

5=Red

6=Black

7=Orange

# Ananias Followed Instructions

## Memory Verse

*You are my friends if you do what I command.* John 15:14

## Obeying God (Acts 9:10–19)

There was a disciple in Damascus named Ananias. God told him in a dream to go to a certain house and look for a man named Saul to heal him of his blindness. Saul was known for hating Christians. Ananias was afraid of Saul. But Ananias didn't realize that Saul's heart was changed. Saul was now a follower of Jesus. Even though Ananias did not know he was a follower of Jesus, he still obeyed God and went to Saul. Color the picture.

# Saul Escaped

## Memory Verse

*Some of the other believers lowered him in a large basket.* Acts 9:25

## Lowered in a Basket (Acts 9:22–25)

Saul followed Jesus and became a Christian! He told Jews living in Damascus that Jesus is the Messiah. There was a conspiracy among the Jews to kill him, but Saul learned of their plan. Day and night, they kept close watch on the city gates in order to kill him. But Saul's friends took him by night and lowered him in a basket through an opening in the wall. Color the picture.

# Dorcas Was a Wonderful Person

## Memory Verse

*[Dorcas] was always doing kind things for others and helping the poor.* Acts 9:36

## Always Helping the Poor (Acts 9:36)

In Joppa, there was a disciple named Dorcas. She was always doing good things and helping the poor. She used to make nice clothing for people. Color the picture.

# Dorcas Was Loved by Many

## Memory Verse

*Let's not get tired of doing what is good. At just the right time we will reap a harvest of blessing if we don't give up.* Galatians 6:9

## Kind Acts (Acts 9:36–39)

Dorcas was a woman who did good deeds for other people. One of her good deeds was making clothing for the poor. One day, Dorcas got sick and died. Her friends called Peter to help. When he arrived, many wept and showed him the clothes Dorcas had made for them.

Decorate the robe that Dorcas made. Color the picture.

# Peter Healed Dorcas

## Memory Verse

*The news spread through the whole town, and many believed in the Lord.* Acts 9:42

## Dorcas Lived Again (Acts 9:40–42)

Peter knew Dorcas's friends were very sad that she died and that they were going to miss her very much. When Peter arrived at Dorcas's house, he had everyone leave the room where she lay. Peter got down on his knees and prayed. Suddenly, Dorcas came to life and sat up! God helped Peter bring Dorcas back from the dead. Color the picture.

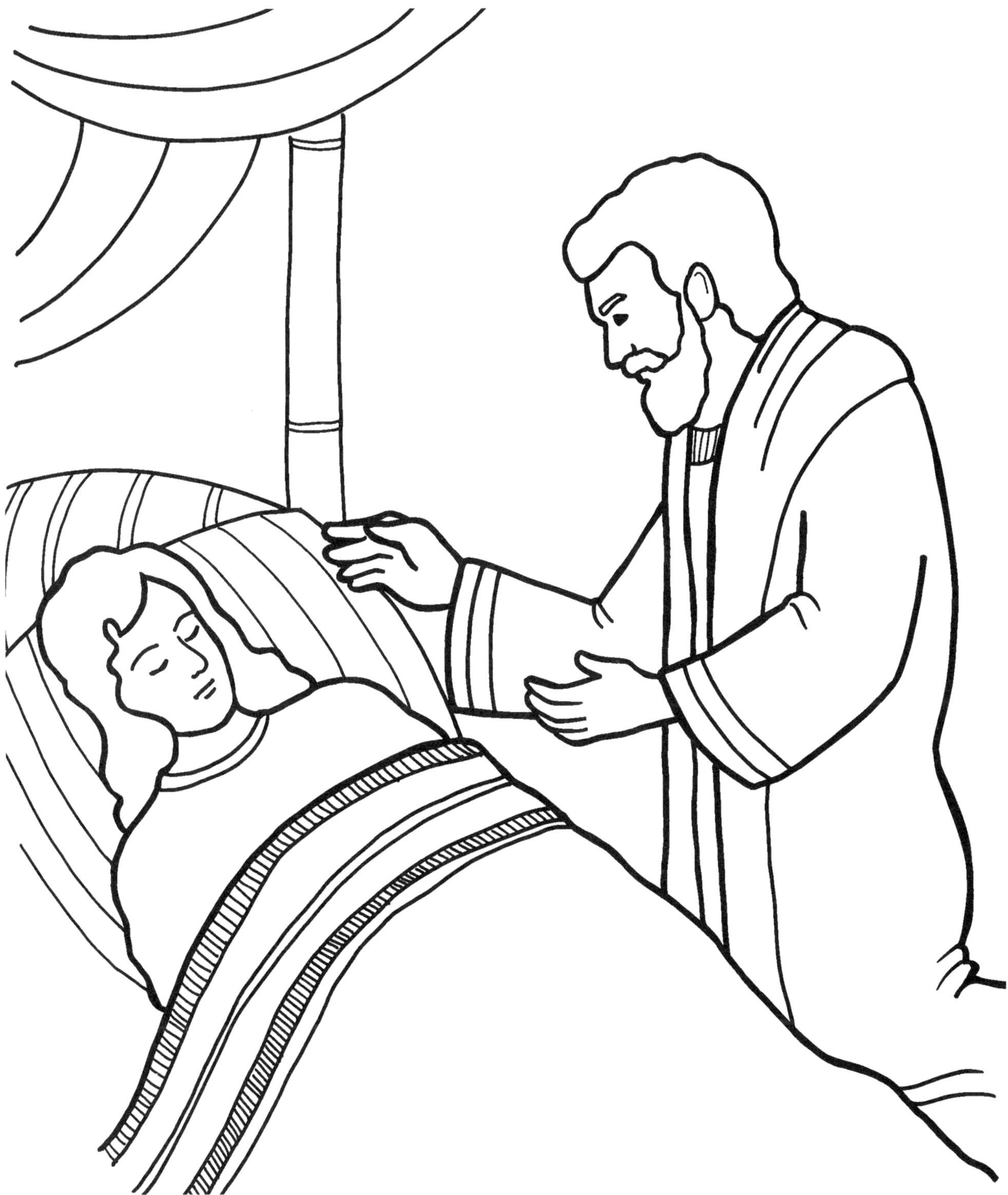

# Peter Entered Mary's House

## Memory Verse

*The Lord had led [Peter] out of prison.* Acts 12:17

## Safety (Acts 12:16–19)

An angel lead Peter out of prison! Peter kept knocking on the door of Mary's house until she finally let him in. Peter's friends were very excited and happy to see him. But Peter quieted them down and told them how the Lord led him to safety. Back at the prison, the guards had no idea what happened to Peter. King Herod searched everywhere for him, but Peter was safe at Mary's house.

Draw wood on the door and a curtain on the window. Color the picture.

# Paul Told about Jesus

## Memory Verse

*We are here to bring you this Good News.* Acts 13:32

## People Who Heard about Jesus (Acts 13:13–51)

Paul traveled all around telling people about Jesus. Sometimes people were happy to hear about Jesus. Other times, they were not. Paul did not let anything stop him from telling people that Jesus would forgive their sins. Paul was one of the first missionaries. Missionaries are people who often go far away to tell others about Jesus.

Look at the picture of Paul preaching to the people. Draw smiles on the people hearing the good news! Color the picture.

# **Lydia** Believed in Jesus

## Memory Verse

*The Lord opened [Lydia's] heart and she accepted what Paul was saying.* Acts 16:14

## **Her Heart** Was Opened (Acts 16:13–15)

The apostles were not allowed to hold prayer meetings in the city of Philippi, so they went to the river to pray. At the river, they sat down and spoke about Jesus to the women who were gathered there. Lydia was one of the women. She sold purple cloth for a living, and she was very wealthy. But even though she was wealthy, she still needed Jesus. Her heart was opened to Paul's teaching. She believed in Jesus and was baptized in the river along with the rest of her family. Color the picture.

# Lydia Shared with Missionaries

## Memory Verse

*Cheerfully share your home with those who need a meal or a place to stay.* 1 Peter 4:9

## Learning More about Jesus (Acts 16:13–15)

Paul, Silas, Timothy, and Luke were missionaries who took the Gospel of Jesus throughout the world. They didn't have hotels like we have today, so they had to rely on other Christians for beds and food. Lydia was a Christian who invited them into her home. She gave them a place to sleep, good food, and friendship. In return, Lydia was blessed because she and her family got to hear more about Jesus while the missionaries were there.

Draw fruit on the table. Color the picture.

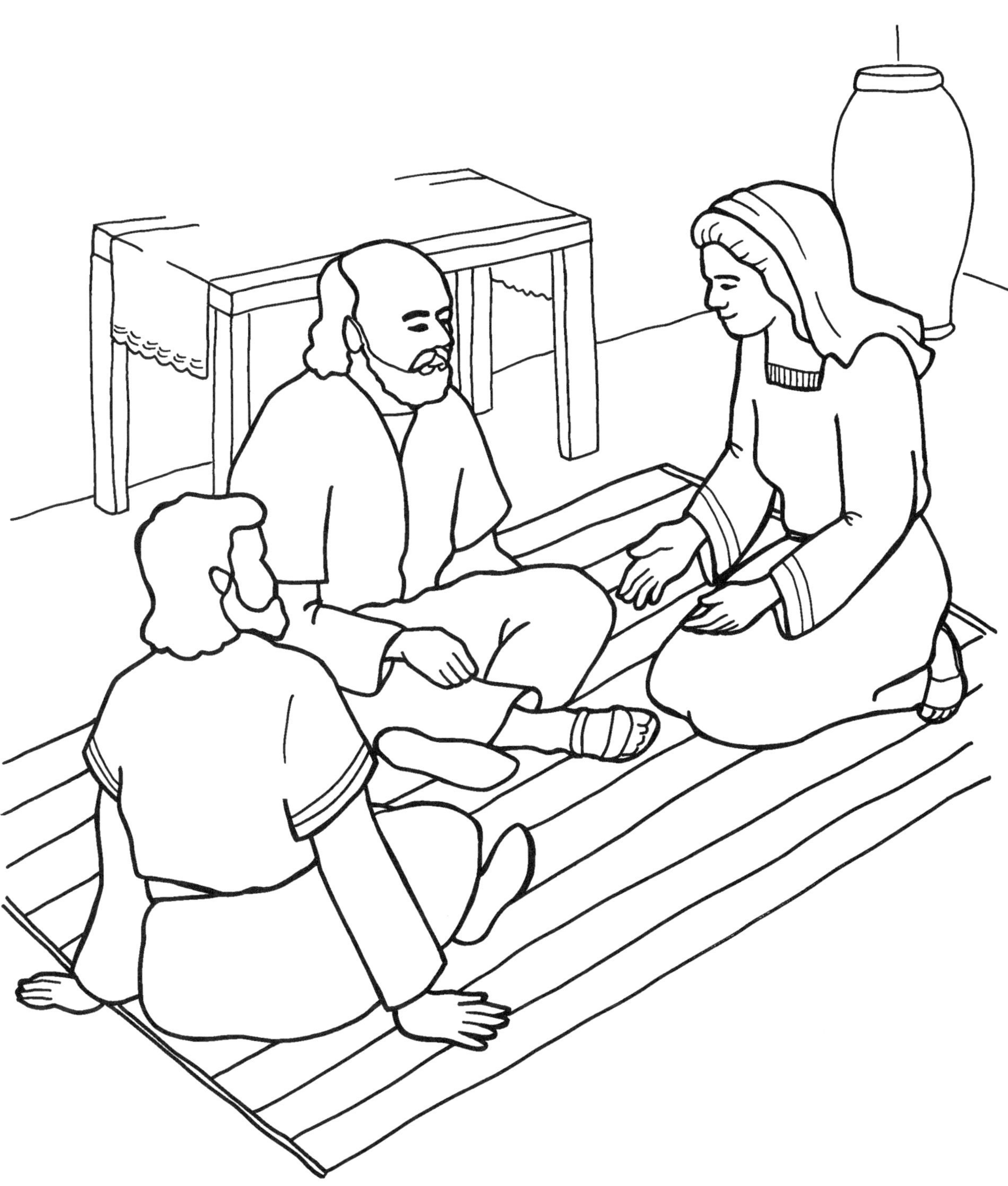

# Paul Told about God

## Memory Verse

*You must not have any other god but me. You must not make for yourself an idol of any kind.* Exodus 20:3–4

## Preaching for the One True God (Acts 17:16–33)

Paul once went to Athens, a city where people worshiped many false gods and idols. Paul told everyone about the one true God.

Cross out all of the idols. Color the picture.

# We Are Children of God

## Memory Verse

*Since we are his children, we are his heirs.* Romans 8:17

## Heirs of God (Romans 8:15–17)

When you become a Christian, you become God's child. You are *heirs* of God. Being an heir means you become part of God's family and you share in the great treasures that he has planned for you. Think of the kinds of treasures that are waiting in heaven for you! Color the picture.

# Jesus Is King of Our Hearts

## Memory Verse

*Christ will be revealed from heaven by the blessed and only almighty God, the King of all kings and Lord of all lords.* 1 Timothy 6:15

## Worship the King

To make Jesus king of our hearts, we have to believe in him and accept the free gift of salvation that he offers us. Then, we will want to please our king, learn from the Bible, and do our best to obey him.

Draw a crown on Jesus' head. Color the picture.